Mary Christmas

short stories spanning two centuries

By

Diane Gustafson

ISBN: 1-4033-1467-5 (Paperback)
ISBN: 1-4033-1466-7 (e-book)

This book is printed on acid free paper.

1stBooks - rev. 08/10/07

for my family:

Bill, Brian, and Danielle

My loving thanks to my husband Bill for his support and to my friends who have read these stories and given encouragement and constructive criticism.

Special thanks go to Faith Scott, my friend for nearly forty years, who painstakingly checked every page of the manuscript at least twice.

I am grateful to Mary Grace, my aunt, who gave me a copy of her husband Sam's letter after his death in 1996 and suggested that I use it in a story. I have taken creative liberty with the circumstances and dialogue, but Sam's poignant letter remains as he wrote it in 1945.

Table of Contents

Going Away

1808

"Oh, Tree, I'm going to miss you."

Molly Campbell leaned against the trunk of the oak and sighed. This had been her special place since childhood. From atop this hill she could look down on the cabins below and to the surrounding forest of oak, hickory, walnut, and chestnut trees. She was close enough to watch family members as they did their chores, yet far away enough to see the entire village. Sometimes she wondered if it were like that for God. Did He watch people on earth going about their work, not seeing what He did, that a storm was coming, that change was coming?

She remembered countless times when she had rested in the shade of this tree in summer, the breeze so cool. In autumn she loved the crackling sound of the fallen colored leaves under her boots. Now she looked up through the bare branches to the bright blue sky on this uncommonly mild December day. There had been only two brief dustings of snow so far that winter. Would there be an early spring? Tears filled her eyes as she realized that she would not be there to see it. In truth, she would not see this tree nor her home ever again. Davey Scott, the man she would marry the day after Christmas, was taking her to Charlotte Town for the winter and then, in the spring, far away, into the new land President Jefferson had purchased from France.

Molly was the fourth generation of women in her family to be named Mary at birth.

The original Mary Campbell had come with her husband to North Carolina from Scotland via Ireland in 1741. She had become a legend in these hills. There were stories telling how she had killed the Indians who tried to burn her house, how she had borne six children and taken in four more orphaned in a massacre.

Mary Campbell's first daughter was named for the mother, and the girl did the same, years later. All four of the orphans named their first daughters for the woman who had raised them. Thus began the tradition and the proliferation of women named Mary.

It was very confusing when the relatives got together. Of course, many of the Marys had different last names, so one could call them "Mary Harper" or "Mary Cameron". Even so, in the close-knit community there was much intermarrying and there were several Mary Campbells, so nicknames came to be used.

One of Molly's brothers called to her from the base of the hill, "Granny Mary wants to see you!"

"I'm coming," the girl answered.

As she started down the path to the village, her boot kicked an acorn that had been overlooked by the squirrels. She picked it up, intending to take it as a reminder of home.

Granny Mary was indeed Molly's grandmother and the daughter of the original Mary Campbell. At sixty she was considered an old woman and had outlived all but one of her six children.

Molly stood in the doorway of the log cabin and, as her eyes adjusted to the dim light, saw Granny Mary in bed under piles of blankets. Wisps of her hair, once as vibrant red as Molly's own but now faded to a rose-gray, appeared from beneath her woolen cap.

"Can't seem to get warm these days," the old woman said. "Come closer so we can have a little talk."

The girl pulled up a stool and took the old, wrinkled hand in her smooth one.

"So you're going away, Child."

"Yes, right after the wedding. Davey has finished his apprenticeship and will work for the gunsmith in Charlotte Town until spring. We'll be able to save some money for our journey."

"You're sure this is what you want?"

"What can I say? I'd rather stay here, but I love him. And he wants to go west."

"I'm afraid for you, Child, afraid there are hard times ahead for you."

"But why?"

"Oh, Davey's a nice enough young man, but I see restlessness in him, just like in Abner."

"Who's Abner?"

"My first husband, Abner MacDonald."

"I never knew you'd been married before Granddaddy. What happened to him?"

"Killed by Indians. And three months it took for me to find out. Abner was always heading out for new adventures, always looking for something better. A good-looking man, could make my heart turn just by looking at me, but he was worthless as a stay-at-home husband. One day he left, said he'd be back in a couple weeks, but weeks turned into months, and then one day a trapper came by and told me Abner was dead."

"Davey won't be like that, Granny. He'll stay put once we have a home and children."

"I fear for you, Molly, and pray I'm wrong. Doubt it, though. I've always been a good judge of character." She chuckled and added, "Except for Abner. Anyway, I'm sorry to see you go. You've always been my favorite. Don't know if I ever told you that. I couldn't love you more if you'd come from my own body. You're the only one of my grandchildren who ever wanted me to teach 'em to read. That's something special between us. It's a mighty good thing knowing how to read, Molly. You can study the Bible and know for yourself what it says instead of taking somebody else's word for it. That's important. You have to teach your children and grandchildren to read. That's why I'm giving you my Bible."

"I can't take it."

"You've got to, Molly. I'm not going to last much longer. When I get up There, the good Lord will give me a new Bible, so I won't be needing this one." She reached beneath her pillow and pulled out a worn volume.

The girl took it and opened it to the middle.

"Psalm 100. That's the first one you taught me. It's still my favorite."

"Mine, too, Child. That's why I picked it. And it was short. Read it to me now."

The old woman's eyes were closed as she listened to the clear, sweet voice.

"Make a joyful noise unto the Lord, all ye lands. Serve the Lord with gladness; come before His presence with singing. Know ye that the Lord He is God; it is He that hath made us, and not we ourselves; we are His people, and the sheep of His pasture. Enter into His gates with thanksgiving, and into His courts with praise; be thankful unto Him, and bless His name. For the Lord is good; His mercy is everlasting; and His truth endureth to all generations."

"Thank you for the Bible, Granny. I'll treasure it

always, and I promise I'll teach my children and grandchildren to read."

"I want you to promise me, too, that you'll carry on the tradition and name your first daughter Mary."

"I will. And Granny…"

"Yes?"

"You're wrong about Davey. He'll change, I know he will."

"Well, now, Molly, if later on he goes off looking for adventure, don't you go complaining to the Lord, 'cause He'll just tell you your granny warned you. Just make as good a home for your children as you can, and for Davey when he's there. Once you make your bed, you have to lie in it. One thing, though, don't let him hit you. A woman doesn't have to stay with a man who hits her. Maybe Reverend MacLeod wouldn't like me saying that, but you remember."

"I will."

"And now, you go on. I know you have a lot to do before you leave, and I need a little sleep."

The girl rose from the stool and kissed the wrinkled cheek. She started to go, then turned back.

"Maybe Davey would be willing to wait awhile to move on. Maybe we could stay the winter here."

"Now why would you do that?"

"I just want to be with you a bit longer, that's all."

"Bless you, Child, that's a sweet thought, but no. You must go."

"It would only be for…"

"No, Molly, I want you to go the day after Christmas, just like you planned. I won't last 'til Spring. Now, don't go getting all teary-eyed on me. I've had a long, good life. I can't wait to get up There to see our Lord, and your granddaddy, and my children. David, Mary, Jonah, Lizzy, Matthew. Only one left down here is your Uncle Samuel. There's a whole lot of loved ones waiting up there for me. I'm ready. But I'd like you to remember me living and breathing, not wrapped in a blanket ready to go into the ground. I want you to go with Davey just like the Psalm says, 'making a joyful noise unto the Lord'. I love you, Molly."

Clutching the Bible, Molly nodded and left the cabin. She sat down on a tree stump and wiped her tears with her sleeve.

She looked up and saw Davey coming through the trees. His copper-colored hair gleamed in the sunlight as he called her name and raised his left hand to show the rabbits he had killed. She remembered what Granny had said about Abner, that he could turn her heart just by looking at her.

"That's the way it is with me and Davey," she whispered. "You're wrong about him, Granny. Once I make him a home and we have a child or two, he'll stop thinking about moving on. He'll be happy just staying put. I know it."

Orphan Train

1857

Nine-year old Moira Brennan first saw New York harbor in June 1857 from the deck of the crowded boat which had brought her family from Ireland. Her brother Sean, just five years old, clutched her hand. Behind her, Da laid his hand on her dark curls and sighed, "We're here at last."

"Wish Mum was here to see it," Moira said.

Mum, pregnant with her third child, had been sick almost from the first day out at sea. As the days passed, she couldn't keep down any food, nor water later on. On the eleventh day she died, and they had wrapped her in a blanket and pushed her overboard. A cruel way to be laid to rest, but Da understood the necessity of it, even if the children could not.

In that same month, June 1857, Lucy Alexander of Springfield, Illinois, gave up praying for a child. Five years they had been married, and if God were going to give her the babies she wanted so desperately, He would have by now, wouldn't He? Each month when she found blood on her underclothes, it felt like a fist in her chest, making it hard for her to breathe. Lately she had decided that the blood came not only from within her private parts but from her heart, her broken and bleeding heart.

Well, she'd have no more of it. The praying, that is. If God wouldn't listen, why should she waste her time talking to Him? She had other things to do. Baking, sewing, helping Jeremiah in the food and dry goods store. And, in fact, she was so busy that she stopped going to church on Sunday mornings. If God could ignore her, she'd ignore God.

Da found a tiny room on the second floor of a crowded building. There were two beds, a small cooking stove, table, and two chairs. A small window looked out on the building next door.

They were luckier than many. Others had been robbed of their meager belongings upon arrival in the harbor. Da had held fast to the two bundles that represented all their possessions. Their clothes in one and in the other their cups and bowls, the family Bible, and a knotted handkerchief that held a clump of earth from their farm in Ireland.

Moira had held Sean's hand in one of hers and with the other she grasped the hem of Da's coat.

It was a noisy place, this New York, and there were strange, sometimes unpleasant smells. But at least it was better than the horrible, crowded ship. Forty-seven days they had been under sail, and Moira promised Sean that they'd never have to get on another boat, no matter what.

Within three days Da found a job at the docks. He left when the sun came up and returned when it was almost dark, six days a week. On Sundays he would take his children to church and then for walks. Moira loved Sundays because, except for Sean, she was lonely much of the time.

Da told them that when he had saved enough money, they would leave New York and go west to a place called Californy, where the streets were made of gold and a man needed to work only nine hours a day.

Moira's time was filled with telling stories to her little brother, stories about long ago in Ireland and about the future in Californy. She made most of it up, and soon the fantasy world she created became their reality. Sean's favorite stories were about a black horse, the shiniest and fastest in all the world, and only Sean could ride him bareback.

They played with the O'Hara children down the hall and went to the market with Mrs. O'Hara because the merchants might have cheated a child with money for shopping. Moira cooked; they ate a lot of soup and bread and drank mostly water.

One night Da didn't come home, and Moira lay awake all night. Not wanting to wake her little brother, she stuffed the edge of the blanket into her mouth to muffle her sobs.

"Where is he?" she cried to Mrs. O'Hara the next morning.

The woman gathered the sobbing child into her arms, and Moira could feel the woman's heart beating almost as wildly as her own.

"When Mr. O'Hara comes home tonight, we'll ask him to go look, but your da will probably return long before that."

"Can't we go look now?" the little girl begged.

So they had all gone to the docks. Mrs. O'Hara and her four children and Moira and Sean.

Jeremiah put his arms through the sleeves of his Sunday-best coat.

"Won't you come to church this week?" he asked.

"No, perhaps next time," Lucy said.

"I don't like this," he said. "I feel like I have to make excuses for you when people ask where you are."

"Then don't tell them anything. It's none of their concern."

He laid his hand on her blonde head. "Of course, they're concerned. They're friends and want to help."

"Nothing and no one can help," she said.

Dead. Da was dead. Moira couldn't believe it. A sack of wheat weighing a hundred pounds had fallen from the ship, crushing him below. He was buried in the cemetery for the poor.

Mr. O'Hara had asked for and received the pay owed to Da. It was enough to last a week, but then the rent on the room would have to be paid. What then?

Moira had overheard the O'Haras talking when they thought she and Sean were asleep.

"We can barely manage with our own four," he told his wife. "We cannot take on two children who aren't even family."

They asked Moira about relatives back in Ireland.

"Ain't nobody. That's why we came here. Ain't nobody back there. 'Sides, me and Sean don't never want to go back on a boat. Never."

Finally the day came when Mrs. O'Hara helped them pack up all their possessions because a man with a big black moustache stood outside the door with another family waiting to come in. Moira looked with longing at the little group, mother, father, and two boys. Family. She started to cry all over again.

Later that morning, Mrs. O'Hara held the two children on her lap and tried to explain what was going to happen.

"Some people are going to come to take you to a new place, an asylum for children with no parents."

"What's asylum?" Moira asked.

"It means a safe place."

Sean sniffled. “I want to stay here!”

Mrs. O’Hara stroked his hair and said, “I wish to Heaven I could keep you, truly I do, but I can’t. But you’ll be all right.”

The asylum was a strange place with children of all ages, some speaking words Moira couldn’t understand. She and Sean shared a small bed in a big room with more children than she could count.

Moira worked part of each day in the kitchen, and Sean’s job was to help set the tables for meals. Unlike many others, they were spared the stick used for punishment, but it was a constant fear.

They were dry when it rained, and they got enough to eat. But there were no hugs, no kisses.

The two children retreated further and further into their fantasy world. Da was already in Californy and would soon come back to get them. There would be gold dust on his boots. And when they got to that wonderful place, he would buy Sean a big, shiny, black horse. They spent hours discussing the name for it. Sean insisted that it be his choice and that Moira could name her own horse.

Jeremiah finished his supper and patted his ample middle. “Fine pie, Lucy.”

She looked down at her hands in her lap.

“You’re so pale,” he said, “and you never smile anymore.”

“I’m sorry, but I just don’t feel like it.”

“Listen,” he said, “I heard some interesting news today. Next week, November 4th to be exact, a train is coming to town. It’s part of the Emigration Plan.”

“What?”

"A train bringing orphans from New York City out here so farm families can adopt them."

"So?"

"Well, what do you think?"

"We're not a farm family, Jeremiah, so what's to think?"

"Mr. Randall down at the bank is the local agent who's going to oversee the distribution, that's what he calls it. He said he doesn't see any reason why we shouldn't be able to have one of the children."

"But these are children, not babies, right?"

He nodded.

"I want a baby."

"But they grow up, Lucy. You'll have missed the baby days, but you'll still have lots of years to love the child."

"I'll think about it," she promised.

On Monday of the following week, as they lay in bed, she whispered, "Are you awake?"

"Yes."

"Do you think we should get a girl or a boy?"

"Does it matter to you?"

"Well, I think I'd rather have a girl. I could sew clothes for her. We got that nice flowered calico in the last shipment. Can we get a girl?"

He was silent for a few seconds, and she said, "You were thinking of a boy, weren't you?"

"Well, yes, I have to admit it. I'd like a boy to take fishing on Sunday afternoons."

"What are we going to do?" she asked.

"I think we should wait 'til the train gets here and see what children they have and decide then."

Springfield was to be the train's next stop. The previous day six of the children had been taken away by families at the depot. But not Moira and Sean.

They sat looking out the window, Sean with his thumb in his mouth. It seemed like the fields were passing the train instead of the other way around. Moira thought it looked a little like the ocean, stretching out as far as the eye could see. She shut her eyes tight to block the image of Mum being pushed over the side of the boat.

Miss Carter, the lady from the Children's Aid Society who was accompanying them on this journey, knelt in the aisle beside them.

"We're coming into another town in a few minutes. Here, let me wash your faces. Maybe this place will be your new home."

Jeremiah and Lucy waited on the platform with the other couples. She stood on her toes and looked down the track. He smiled, and she wrinkled her forehead. "I'm trying not to get my hopes up," she whispered.

Mr. Randall spoke in a loud voice. "Catholic children will be down at that end and Protestant children over here. Adoptions will only be permitted by their own kind. When, if, you find the child of your choice, raise your hand, and I'll come right over."

Sean was squeezing her hand so hard that Moira thought her thumb would come off. She patted his head and whispered soothingly.

A tall man in a funny hat and checkered coat and a woman with yellow hair and a purple dress came toward the children at the Catholic end of the platform.

They looked at each child and spoke to most of them.

"And what's your name?" the man asked Sean.

The boy kept his thumb in his mouth and moved closer to his sister.

"It's Sean," Moira replied.

"You're Irish, I suspect," the man said.

Moira nodded.

He knelt down so that his face was right next to Sean's and he asked, "Would you like to come home with us?"

The boy looked in terror at Moira.

"He won't go nowhere without me," she said.

"But we can give him a good home. You won't have to worry about that."

"He won't go nowhere without me, and I won't go without him. We're all we got."

The woman in the purple dress was pulling her husband away. Moira's heart was heavy because this was yet another stop where they'd have to get back on the train, but at least she and her brother would be together. Suddenly fear washed over her, and she began to shiver. It had never occurred to her that she and Sean might be separated.

She glanced down the platform and saw five of the Protestant children being led away by new families.

But, wait! The man in the checkered coat and the lady in the purple dress were coming back. He knelt down again.

"If we took you both, would you like to come with us?"

Moira looked at Sean, who hesitated and then nodded his head slightly. She turned to the man.

"Yes," she said.

The man raised his right hand high into the air.

They all got into a wagon pulled by a brown horse, and within minutes they were in front of a store and then going up the stairs inside.

"Are you hungry?" Lucy asked.

"We could eat some," Moira said.

Lucy looked on as the children nibbled her fried chicken and sipped their milk, all the while their eyes darting about the kitchen. Then they had seconds of everything. Moira answered questions politely, both for herself and her brother.

"Can you not talk, Sean?" Lucy finally asked.

"He don't say much when he's scared," the little girl said.

"Well, you don't have to be scared. Nothing's going to happen to you."

Moira shuddered and swallowed before whispering, "Da said the same thing the first day he left to work on the docks."

Jeremiah brought bucket after bucket of warm water and filled a tub in the kitchen. Lucy scrubbed the two children with nice-smelling soap and pulled soft nightshirts over their heads.

She led them to a little room off the kitchen and pointed to two bedrolls on the floor.

"We didn't have time to get beds for you, but we will soon, and we'll leave a light in the kitchen so you won't be afraid."

During the night Lucy got up three times to check on them. The first time she noticed that Sean had crawled into Moira's bedroll. They were sleeping so close together that they looked like one fused body.

After several days, Lucy realized that the children never called her and Jeremiah by any names. Her eyes filled with tears when she overheard Moira refer to "the lady and the man".

Lucy and Jeremiah spent hours wrestling with the problem of what to have the children call them. "Mr. and Mrs. Alexander"? Too formal. "Lucy and Jeremiah"? Out of the question. Mr. Randall suggested "Mother and Father", but that seemed premature. Finally they asked Moira herself to help them decide.

"Don't know," she replied. "I'll think on it."

The children spent their days helping in the store. Moira counted things. "The man called it inventory," she explained to her brother.

Sean had a little feather duster and brushed things with it. In the first week, he accidentally knocked over a glass jar of sweets. His eyes were wide with fear, and he burst into tears.

Before Moira could cross the store to reach him, the lady and the man took him into their arms and whispered soothing words, assuring him that the wrapped candies were not damaged, even though the container lay shattered, and that he would not be punished.

Moira stood there, watching the scene and feeling jealous. For so long, she had been everything to Sean.

The lady turned and reached out to her.

"Come here, Darling."

Moira walked to the three of them and was pulled into the embrace they shared. She breathed a sigh. She was now the protected rather than the protector. They were safe.

That day at supper, after a discussion with Sean, Moira told the couple that they would call them "Mama and Papa", like children who came into the store called their own parents. This would please the couple, the little girl decided, and yet it took nothing away from the memories of Da and Mum.

She and Sean were warm and well-fed. Mama and Papa were kind to them, to be sure. They hugged and kissed the children, played games with them, took them to church. Moira didn't know what to make of it; she didn't know if Da and Mum up in Heaven would mind. There was no one to tell her. Mr. Randall came by at least once a week and spoke to the two children in private, to be sure they were doing well. And were they happy? Moira never knew what to say.

The third weekend after the arrival of the children, Lucy left the store on Saturday afternoon to go to confession and to make her peace with God.

"Bless me, Father, for I have sinned…" she began, and out poured the story, all the times she had stayed home from Mass, the times she had gone to sleep without saying her prayers.

"And are you truly contrite?" the priest asked.

"Yes. Oh, yes. I know now that I gave up too soon. God did answer my prayers. Just not as fast as I wanted Him to."

"Yes, that's right. Perhaps He knew those children would be needing a home and He was saving you for them."

Lucy walked home from church with a light step and heart filled with joy.

Mr. Randall had told the adoptive families that it would be better not to ever mention the deceased parents, that the children should be allowed to forget them.

At first Lucy and Jeremiah followed this advice, but they became aware that the children whispered at night for a long time before falling asleep. Eavesdropping from the kitchen, Lucy learned of Californy and the black horse. She realized that they were never going to forget their other family, and, surprisingly, she accepted it. After all, she reasoned, if she were the dead mother, it would comfort her not to be forgotten. And so the couple encouraged Moira and Sean to talk about Ireland and Da and Mum. In time the children, no longer having to keep their feelings hidden, began to brighten a bit, and they brought out the clump of earth from the faraway farm. Jeremiah found a pot for the soil, and they watered it until it softened. In the spring, he promised, they would choose a flowering plant for it.

On Christmas morning, the family dressed for church in their new clothes. Sean insisted on taking his gift, a black toy horse, with him. Moira reluctantly left her new doll at home because she was afraid it would start to snow and ruin the yellow hair.

They walked to church, where they sang carols and heard the Christmas story from the priest. Moira held Mama's hand all during the Mass. She decided that she had never known anyone who smiled as much as Mama.

On the way home they met Mr. Randall and his family, and, as always, he took the two little ones aside and asked how they were being treated. The children told him about their Christmas presents.

Once again he asked if they were happy. Moira frowned and whispered, "Do you think Da and Mum would mind? If we was happy, I mean."

He took off his hat and scratched his head. "I'm sure they loved both of you very much, and loving parents always want their children to be happy. You are, kinda, aren't you?"

"Yes, I think that being here with Mama and Papa is the second-bestest place to be. Right, Sean?"

"Right," he said with a smile.

The Gift

1858

Mary Clare stared out the hotel window at Philadelphia below. She didn't remember much about it even though she had spent the first thirteen years of her life in the city.

The bedroom door opened, and Esther came in, carrying Mary Clare's jewel case.

"What are you wearing tonight?"

"The garnets, I think, don't you, Esther?"

Mary Clare watched as her slave removed the necklace, matching earbobs, and bracelet from the box.

Esther was nineteen years old, the same age as Mary Clare, but luck, or rather lack of it, had shaped a different life. While one had been born into a prosperous family living in a three-story house, the other had been born in a drafty cabin with a dirt floor on the plantation called Tranquility, north of Baton Rouge. One had learned to speak French and play the piano; the other picked cotton and later washed dishes in her master's kitchen.

But bad luck had visited the rich girl, too. Six years ago, a fire had destroyed the Philadelphia house and taken the lives of Mary Clare's mother, father, and baby brother. Almost before she knew what was happening, a distant relative of her mother had arrived to take her home to live with him and his family at Tranquility. A family which included Aunt Ellen and three sons, two of whom were in Europe for a year's travel on what they called "the Grand Tour".

Esther lifted Mary Clare's brown hair to fasten the necklace which sparkled against the gold satin bodice.

"Oh, Esther, I'm so happy I could burst!" She looked lovingly at the diamond wedding band which she had been wearing for just three weeks. "And soon we'll be living in London!"

"Never thought I'd be living in London, I can tell you that," Esther said, and she shivered.

And perhaps you never will, Mary Clare thought. Even though I know it's the right thing to do, it would break my heart.

She sat in the upholstered chair next to the window so she could see the lights coming on in the buildings nearby. When Andrew returned, they would go to dinner downstairs in the hotel dining room, but first they would have to talk to Esther.

Mary Clare closed her eyes and remembered that first Christmas at Tranquility when Uncle Henry had said with pride, "And here's your Christmas present." Opening the door of the parlor, he had pulled the hand of a scrawny black girl and pushed her toward Mary Clare.

"I don't understand," Mary Clare had said.

"Her name's Esther, and she's your personal slave. She's yours to keep, to own."

"No! I don't want her! I can't own another human being! Take her away!"

The black girl had looked shocked and began to sniffle, then ran out of the room.

Uncle Henry had spoken slowly, as though it were difficult to keep from showing his anger. "I am going to overlook this outburst because I know how different our life here is for you. I want you to go to your room and to reflect upon your lack of tact and graciousness in refusing our gift to you. And I shall expect an apology for embarrassing me."

She had cried into her pillow for a long time before Aunt Ellen came and stroked her hair.

"I know. This is all so hard for you. Your papa's views on slavery were so different from ours. But try to see your Uncle Henry's point of view. It's what we've grown up with all our lives. Our slaves are well taken care of. They are fed and clothed and seen by the doctor when they are sick. There are many people up North who don't fare nearly as well. You have embarrassed your uncle, Mary Clare, and you have been ungracious in refusing his gift."

"But how can I own that girl?"

"Think of it this way. Esther will have a much better life taking care of you than working in the kitchen. She's a bright girl and pleasant-natured. You'd be doing her a favor in taking her as your personal maid."

"I hadn't thought of it that way."

"Now, dry your eyes and go apologize to your uncle. He loves you, my dear, and he isn't going to bite."

Telling Uncle Henry she was sorry wasn't nearly as hard as she had feared. He immediately pulled her onto his lap and kissed her cheek. "We'll say no more about it," he whispered.

While Mary Clare waited for her husband, Esther was also remembering the years at Tranquility. Life as maid to the master's niece had been good. She slept in the Big House in a tiny room next to Mary Clare's and travelled to Baton Rouge and New Orleans.

Esther remembered that first Christmas, when Miss Mary Clare made a scene by refusing to take Esther as her maid. No one ever apologized to a slave, yet the master's niece had done just that.

Over the years the two young women had become friends. Mary Clare taught Esther to read, although they kept it a secret, and supplied her with books.

Esther always called her mistress "Miss Mary Clare" in public but couldn't bring herself to drop the "Miss" in private, no matter how many times Mary Clare encouraged her to do so. The young lady of the house might be reckless, but Esther had much more to lose. She gave her friendship slowly, cautiously.

Esther knew, long before Master Henry and Miss Ellen, that Mary Clare had fallen in love with Andrew Hamilton, the museum curator from London who was touring the river plantations. She wasn't at all surprised the night Mary Clare confided that Andrew was going to ask Uncle Henry for her hand in marriage. Esther lay in bed in her tiny room for hours, wondering what England was like. She even fantasized that the master would give her the choice of remaining at Tranquility or going with her mistress across the ocean. What would she say? Could she leave her mother and aunts and cousins? The master was far kinder than other plantation owners. He didn't allow slaves to be sold if it meant breaking up families. Surely he wouldn't force her to leave.

Silly girl, she chided herself. Nobody is going to give you the choice. You'll go with your mistress and her husband and be happy to be with people who will treat you right.

Andrew returned with a scroll in his hand.

"That's it?" his wife asked.

He nodded and smiled.

They called Esther into the room. Mary Clare was

silent until Andrew, laughing, said to her, "Well, get on with it! You're the one to tell her."

She began, "Esther, we've been together a long time now."

"Six years."

"It was hard for me to get used to the idea of having a slave."

"You've always been good to me."

"I've been thinking about this for a long time, almost from the beginning. This is a writ of manumission. It means that you're free."

Esther's jaw dropped.

"How can you do that?" she asked.

"Uncle Henry said you were mine to keep. 'To own' was the way he put it. I can do whatever I want with you, and I choose to set you free. I couldn't do it before, not at Tranquility. Not only because of the law but because it would hurt his feelings, Uncle Henry's, I mean. But now that we're here, it doesn't matter. Actually, he need never know."

Esther looked at the offered scroll.

"Go on, take it, Esther," Andrew said. "Think of this as our Christmas gift to you."

"But what would I do? I mean, where would I go?"

Mary Clare bit her lip. "Well, I don't think you could go back South. You could stay here in Philadelphia, maybe work as a lady's maid for wages. We could help you find a job. You're free; you can go almost anywhere."

Esther lowered her eyes and a small tear trickled down her cheek.

"Or you could come to London with us, for wages, of course. I know you're afraid of being on the ocean for such a long time. I'm nervous about it, too. But please say you will. We won't have as much money as Uncle Henry, and you might have to be both maid and nursemaid later on, but we'd like you to be part of our family."

Mary Clare breathed a sigh of relief when Esther raised her eyes and smiled broadly.

"Miss Mary Clare, that's what I want to do."

"Esther, first thing you're going to have to do is drop the 'Miss'. We're going into this great new adventure together."

For Remembrance

1863

The gray stone house sat at the top of a hill outside the western Pennsylvania town of Canonsburg. In the front yard there were lilac bushes and peach and apple trees, and from the sturdiest tree hung a child's swing.

The house, built in 1830, had only four rooms, but they were large. Each room had windows on at least two sides for plenty of light and air. Downstairs, a big kitchen with a fireplace and a table with six chairs. And a parlor with once-fine furniture now showing the wear and tear of little children. A piano stood along one wall, and there was a vacant corner where the Christmas tree would have been. Upstairs were the parents' bedroom and the nursery, but the latter had no mattresses on the beds and no toys in the corners.

It was the home of Dr. James Harrison and his wife, Marianne. James was on the personal staff of General George Meade and had not been home since shortly after the Federal Army's victory at Gettysburg.

Marianne, her strawberry-blonde hair matted and uncombed, stood at the kitchen door, looking out over the back yard. Baby ducks were swimming in a large puddle created by the recent rains. Beyond were the barn and chicken house, and farther still, at the edge of the woods, was a mound of earth and beneath it her three children.

"I wish the fever had taken me, too," she sobbed.

Pete, the old bloodhound, licked her hand as though he knew how much she needed comforting.

Her parents had urged her to come into town with them to spend Christmas, but she had refused. She said she wanted to stay in her own house in case James came home, but the truth was that she couldn't bear to be around anyone, not even her parents.

No mother should ever outlive her children, she thought. And then she remembered Mary, whose Son was born this day so many years ago. She probably didn't think she would outlive Him. But she had had thirty-three years of loving Jesus. Marianne's little ones had been only six, five, and two.

She threw another log on the fire and reached for pen and ink. If her telegram hadn't brought James home, what use was a letter? Still, she felt he should know about the funeral.

She wasn't sure where James was right then, but surely the Army could find General Meade's headquarters, and he would be there.

Dear James,

The children were buried yesterday. In one large coffin so they will always be together. We put them into the ground beyond the chicken house, near the walnut trees. It started to rain before dawn, a cold, cold rain. It came down hard as though the heavens had opened up and let out the tears of all the angels, crying for our children. It looked at first as though the funeral would have to be postponed, but by mid-morning it was only a drizzle, so we went ahead with it.

In the afternoon Mama and Papa helped me burn everything, all the children's clothes and toys, all the bed linens and mattresses. And so now I not only don't have my children, I don't have things to remember them by. Not that I am ever likely to forget.

I don't understand why God allowed my babies to die. I'm trying to make some sense of it. Today I read again the story of David and Bathsheba and the death of their first son. The child died because David took a married woman to his bed and then allowed her husband to be killed in order to hide David's sin. Try as I might, I cannot relate this to our lives. But then, we are not as close as we once were, are we, James? Would I even know if you had sinned in a way that God would punish us all for?

I do not think the children were in pain. It happened quickly. They were fine last week and now they are gone. They were all delirious. Jimmy kept calling for you, "Papa, come home!" Little Mary thought she was on the swing. "Higher!" she would cry. John was quiet in my arms, except for occasional whimpering.

Do you have any idea what it did to me to have to go through this alone? Why didn't you come when I sent you the telegram telling you how deathly ill your children were? Could you not have come for their funeral?

I hate this war! I hate what it has done to us, to our family. I hate your sense of duty that extends to General Meade and President Lincoln but never manages to sift down to your family. I hate the way you can push me to the back of your mind, and yes, I hate you, James Harrison. I hate you! God forgive me but I hate you.

A tear rolled down her cheek and fell on the word "forgive", smearing it.

She put her head down on the table and cried. She wanted desperately to be consoled.

Finally, she raised her head and dried her eyes. She read the letter through and then slowly, deliberately, tore it in half, then in half again and again. When the pieces could not be torn further, she swept them into her skirt and tossed them into the fireplace. She went upstairs and lay on the bed, crying herself to sleep.

James came home the next day.

Marianne was sitting in the rocking chair in the children's room, staring out the window into the back yard. Pete lay beside her. She thought back to all of the torment the old dog had endured as playful children had pulled his ears, sat on him, hit him on the nose.

"You miss them, too, don't you, Pete?" she whispered, and he looked up at her with sad eyes.

She heard the sound of a horse's hoofs, then the front door opening and her husband's voice calling her name. The dog stood up and went to the top of the stairs, as though the voice were familiar to him but barely. He barked at his master.

Suddenly James was standing in the doorway, filling it. She had almost forgotten how big he was.

His eyes darted around the room, lingering on the empty bed frames. He knew.

She didn't get up, didn't run to him, just raised her chin, a defiant little gesture as if to say, I won't let you hurt me again.

He came to her and sank to his knees. He was pale and looked very tired, and his eyes were red and swollen. His lower lip quivered.

"I just got the telegram last night. I…I…"

He began to cry, his whole body heaving. He clutched her knees and buried his face in her skirt, which was soon wet with his tears.

Hesitantly, she raised her hand and stroked his dark hair. She didn't hate him anymore, did she ever, really?

"Hush, hush, my darling," she whispered.

Two days later, as they lay in their bed, James ran his hand over her protruding stomach.

"I'm glad this baby is still safe," he said, his voice cracking. "And I promise you I'll be back for the birth in April, even if I have to desert. Have you given any thought to names?"

"For a boy, I don't know. Would you like James again? People do that, you know. Name a second child after the father if the first one dies."

"No. There can never be another Jimmy."

"It doesn't matter because I think this one is going to be a girl, and I want to name her Rosemary. For remembrance. Remembrance of the brothers and sister she'll never know."

"I like that. But let's give her a second name, too. Hope. Hope that the war will end and that we will never again suffer like this."

Postscript: Rosemary Hope Harrison was born on April 15, 1864, and, during her first birthday celebration, word came that President Abraham Lincoln had been killed by an actor. Rosemary moved to South Dakota as a young bride and lived there until her death in 1950. Three of her children were named Jimmy, Mary, and John. For remembrance.

Army Wife

1870

Mariah Hadley thought she knew what she was in for when she married an Army officer.

Her father had made the Army his career, rising to the rank of captain. From the age of sixteen, when her mother died, Mariah had taken care of his house on whatever post he was assigned. She was an accomplished pianist and singer and could make an elegant dinner from whatever was available. She was a true companion to her father, always willing to listen to him talk about his day. As she approached her twentieth birthday, she knew that the day would come when she would marry, but she tried not to think about it. She couldn't bear to leave her beloved papa.

But he left her. One night they had been singing around the piano, and the next morning he wouldn't wake up.

The funeral was, of necessity, hasty because of the hundred-degree heat at Fort Hays. That entire summer was oppressively hot in Kansas.

What to do? Where to go? Mariah had an elderly great-aunt in Detroit. Could she go there? It was all happening too fast!

But Libbie Custer and her husband, General George Armstrong Custer, offered a bed in their home next door until she could decide what to do. The Custers always had visitors, usually young women to keep Libbie company.

Mariah and her father had liked the couple very much. Despite his true rank of Lieutenant Colonel, Custer was addressed as "General", his brevet rank from the recent war, by those who liked him. Those who didn't like him called him unrepeatable names behind his back.

Captain Hadley had been dead only three weeks when Captain Zachary Phillips, a widower, arrived to take his place at the fort and to occupy his house. He was a fine-looking man, very tall and muscular, with graying dark hair and hazel eyes. He towered over Mariah, but she thought he was the kindest, gentlest man she had ever met. He taught her to play backgammon and seemed the essence of patience. When he asked her to marry him, just two months after their first meeting, she wept with pleasure and considered herself the luckiest of women.

"Are you sure you're not rushing things?" Libbie had asked. "You know you can stay with us as long as you want. Perhaps you should take more time, get to know him better."

"I know him well enough to know he'll make me happy. It's such a relief not to have to make decisions about the future. And I'll be living in my old house again. What marvelous luck!"

The wedding was held on the first of October. Mariah wore a sapphire blue satin gown that brought out the blue of her eyes, and Libbie twisted her own pink silk roses into a coronet for the bride's blonde hair.

Zachary promised her a real honeymoon the following spring and spent hours telling her about exciting places he had been. New Orleans, New York, Philadelphia. He would take her to the city of her choice.

Mariah was happy except for one thing. Two things, really. Zachary drank too much, and he got very angry when she suggested that he drank too much.

Her father had enjoyed a glass of wine with dinner a couple of times a week and occasionally a brandy while they played chess. But she had never seen him drunk. And she knew that General Custer never touched liquor at all.

As the weather grew colder and the days shorter, Zachary became more restless. There would be no more forays against the Indians for months. He hated the flat landscape, the absence of trees. He hadn't expected it to be this cold in Kansas. He couldn't stand his wife's attempts to cheer him up, and if she said just one more time, "Before you know it, it'll be spring!"...

On the first nice day after a particularly bad snowstorm, most of the men mounted their horses and headed out of the fort. Libbie pulled on her coat and boots and walked the short distance to the Phillips house. She hadn't seen Mariah in nearly a week.

After the third knock, Mariah opened the door a crack.

"I've missed seeing you! I'll come in and we'll have a nice, long chat," Libbie said.

But the door remained open only a few inches.

"I'm sorry, Libbie. I can't ask you in. I have a terrible headache. In fact, I've been in bed since yesterday."

"I'll go home and get my lavender oil. When you rub it on your temples, it's guaranteed to cure headaches. I'll be back in five minutes."

"No! I mean, please don't go to the trouble. I just need some quiet. Please go. I'll come over and see you soon."

The next time the officers' wives got together, Mariah seemed quieter and looked paler. Libbie smiled, anticipating a announcement from her friend about a coming baby, but Mariah said nothing.

In December the entire command began to plan for Christmas. The women gathered to make decorations for the social hall and toys for the children. Mariah came rarely, and the women were never invited to her home. Still, Libbie assumed that she was pregnant and not feeling well. Perhaps she was waiting until the morning sickness and danger of miscarriage had passed before making the announcement.

On Christmas Eve the men and children were hanging the decorations, and the women were in their own kitchens, gathering the foods each had made for the feast. Mariah sent her apple pies on ahead with Zachary and came to Libbie's so they could go together to the party.

Libbie put on her cape and adjusted her warm hood.

"I'll get the baked beans, Mariah, and you take the potatoes. They're in that pan on the table. My goodness," Libbie laughed, "you're a million miles away! Come on, get the potatoes."

"They look heavy, Libbie. Maybe we should get one of the men to help us."

"They're not that heavy. I could pick them up myself if I weren't carrying the beans."

Mariah went to the table and picked up the pan. Libbie saw her wince and drop it. Three potatoes rolled onto the floor.

"What is it?" Libbie asked.

"Nothing. I'm sorry I'm so clumsy."

"You are not clumsy. I can tell you're in pain. What's going on?"

Libbie tugged at her friend's cape until it fell to the floor. She reached for the woman's left arm. Gently, she unbuttoned Mariah's sleeve, pushed it up, and gasped. The entire arm was black and blue and swollen.

Their eyes met.

"Please don't ask me any questions," Mariah pleaded.

"I don't have to. How long has this been going on?"

"Almost from the beginning. He gets drunk and angry and hits me and then he's sorry. He promises it'll never happen again, but it does."

"Why didn't you tell me?"

"I was ashamed. And he said that if I told it could damage his career."

"You cannot go on like this."

"I have no choice, Libbie." Her lip trembled. "Promise me you won't say anything."

"I promise I won't let on to Zachary that I know."

But Libbie hadn't promised not to tell her own husband. The next morning after they opened their presents to each other, Libbie told him about Mariah.

"What can we do?" she asked him.

"We? Not much. We haven't seen him do anything. Besides, if he finds out we know, he'll take his anger out on her."

"But can't you do something? Send him out on a dangerous mission?"

"Libbie! Surely you're not suggesting such a thing! And even if I were agreeable, it's winter. There are no campaigns against the Indians, won't be 'til spring. No, about the only thing we can do is try to keep her close to us as much as possible and let her know that she can turn to us for help when she needs it. I'm glad you invited them for Christmas dinner."

"Why do you think they asked us, Mariah?"

"Well, Libbie is my best friend here, and this is your first Christmas on the frontier."

"It's awkward having dinner with your commanding officer, and Custer is so condescending, doesn't touch a drop of liquor, probably won't even have wine with dinner. I'll just have a drink or two before we go."

Mariah bit her lower lip and said nothing.

Zachary's two drinks turned into half a dozen, and by dinner time he was snoring loudly in front of the fire. Mariah considered not going, saying she didn't feel well, but her loyalty to her husband was wearing thin and she had looked forward so much to this Christmas dinner. She thought of waking him, but, frankly, she found it more pleasant to let him sleep. She decided to go alone. To her relief, neither Custer asked for an explanation. Perhaps they had guessed and wanted to spare her the humiliation.

The three of them were just starting the main course when there was a knock on the front door. Libbie's maid led Zachary into the dining room. "My apologies, Sir," he said, "my wife failed to wake me from a nap." He glowered at Mariah, who looked down at her hands in her lap.

The next hour passed pleasantly. Zachary seemed perfectly normal, didn't slur his words, didn't seem to have had anything to drink. But Mariah was afraid, afraid of what he would say when they got home. She wished the night would never end.

But it did.

Zachary politely helped her on with her coat and repeated effusive apologies to his host and hostess for his late arrival and thanks for the invitation. As they walked out the front door, his hand was very firmly planted on the back of his wife's neck, and she looked terrified.

Not a word was said on the short walk back to their home. Once inside, he poured himself a drink, drained the glass and then another. She took off her cape and stood there, not knowing what to do or say. Finally, he crossed the room, looked down at her, and slapped her face hard.

"How dare you humiliate me in front of my commanding officer like that! I would think that the daughter of an Army officer would know how the game is played. What are you trying to do, ruin my career? Don't forget, Madam, if I go down, you go with me!"

The power of his slap had caused her to reel backward, and she tripped over a footstool, tumbling to the floor. He kicked her and continued to shout.

She was crying as she struggled to get up, and he kicked her again. He was coming at her, towering over her, his eyes wild with rage. She backed toward the fireplace, and he kept coming. She looked down and saw the poker, picked it up in her right hand. He grabbed it from her and held it over her as she cowered.

"Put it down, Captain!" General Custer said from the doorway.

Zachary turned, poker still in hand. "I didn't hear

you knock."

"I didn't."

Mariah clutched her side where Zachary had kicked her.

Custer said, "Go to my house. Now!"

She limped toward the door.

Zachary addressed his commanding officer. "Now, Custer, you know how it is. They need a little scare now and then to keep 'em in line. How about a drink, just this once? It's Christmas."

"Colonel Custer to you, and you know I don't drink. You look like you've had enough already. Now put the poker down."

"And if I don't?"

"I said, put it down. Now!"

Zachary took one step toward the door, poker raised menacingly.

Custer threw himself at the larger man, tackling him in the stomach and causing the poker to fall to the floor. Zachary brought his fist down hard on Custer's back, knocking him flat.

Mariah froze. Her heart went out to this man who had tried to help her and who was now at the mercy of her drunken husband. She didn't know what to do. Should she run and save herself? Should she try to help the General?

Zachary glared at her. "And as for you, Madam…"

He bent to retrieve the poker, dropping it twice, and all she could think of was that he would surely kill her. She couldn't outrun him. She picked up the first thing she saw, one of the bottles of whiskey on the sideboard, took a step toward him, and hit him, hard, on the side of the head. He lost his balance, tumbled sideways, and his head hit the cast iron stove. He sank to the floor, and a pool of dark liquid began to form under his head.

She screamed. Time seemed to stand still, and then Libbie appeared in the doorway, just as General Custer sat up.

"Are you all right?" Libbie asked her husband.

"Yes, I think so. Just had the wind knocked out of me."

The three of them stared at Zachary's lifeless form. Libbie stepped forward and felt for his pulse.

"Is he…?" Mariah asked.

"Yes."

Mariah stood trembling.

"You're coming home with us, Dear," Libbie said. "It's over. He'll never hurt you again."

Trouble Times Three

1880

They were awake.

Three sets of little feet clumping down the stairs, three voices chattering. Ricky, Daniel, and Gregory, ages seven, five, and three, had napped for only an hour.

With a sigh, Maribel put aside her book, a birthday present from her parents. *The Adventures of Tom Sawyer* by Mr. Twain.

"We're hungry," the two older boys said.

"Yeah, hungwy," Gregory chimed in.

She poured glasses of milk and opened the tin containing the Christmas cookies they had all decorated the day before.

"Can we go outside?" Ricky asked.

Maribel considered the prospect of a few more minutes to read.

"Yes, but you have to stay in the back yard. And don't get into trouble. If you do, Santa Claus might not come."

The sun was shining in San Diego, and the boys needed only sweaters on this day before Christmas. She remembered last year in St. Louis, snow on the ground and the pond frozen. They had only been here in California for three months, but already she wouldn't want to live anywhere else.

She made herself a cup of tea, checked the roast in the oven, and opened the book.

She hadn't finished the chapter when there was a knock on the door. Mrs. Barnes from down the street stood on the porch.

"Now, Mrs. Todd," she began, "I don't want you to panic, that would be the worst thing. But do you know where your boys are?"

"In the back yard," Maribel said, and at that moment she heard her youngest crying.

"Mrs. Todd, two of your boys are on the roof."

"On the roof?!" Maribel shrieked and started to run.

"No, no, you mustn't startle them! They could fall! You must be calm. Do you understand? Calm."

Maribel took a deep breath and walked into the back yard, with Mrs. Barnes close behind. Sure enough, Ricky and Daniel were up on the roof, and Gregory stood below, crying in frustration, "Wanna go too!"

Maribel picked him up and asked, in as composed a manner as she could, "What are you doing, Boys?" Turning to her neighbor, she whispered, "Go find a ladder."

"We wanted to see if Santa Claus could fit down our chimney," Ricky answered.

"Oh? And can he?" Maribel asked.

"Well, it's not very big but I guess he can make it."

"How did you get up there?"

"We climbed on the fence first and then grabbed that pipe thing under the roof."

"My, aren't you clever. But I think it's time for you to come down. It isn't fair for you to be having all that fun and poor little Gregory is stuck down here on the ground. Mrs. Barnes has gone for a ladder, but until she comes back I want you to stay very still and lean over the chimney so you won't fall. Can you do that?"

"Yes, Mum," they said in unison.

It seemed forever until her neighbor returned. Maribel filled the time by telling the boys the story of the first Christmas.

Mrs. Barnes came running up the street and plopped at Maribel's feet. Out of breath, she could barely get out the words, "No ladder."

Maribel pulled her to her feet and pushed her toward the house.

"Boys, I'll just be a minute. See if you can remember the presents the Wise Men brought. And don't let go of the chimney!"

Ignoring Gregory's cries, she deposited him in his crib. Then she and Mrs. Barnes pulled the mattress from her bedroom, struggling until it finally lay on the ground next to the house.

Who should go first? Ricky was older, and this had probably been his idea. He should have to stay up there longer. But Daniel needed his older brother's example in order to jump.

"Ricky," she said, "I want you to sit down on the roof and very carefully slide over to this corner. Daniel, you hold onto the chimney and watch. Your turn will be next."

Ricky did as he was told for a change and soon was sitting on the edge of the roof, his feet dangling.

"Now jump, Darling, and I'll catch you," she said as she stood in the middle of the mattress.

He jumped, and the force of it caused her to topple backward. They both laughed, the boy because it was a new game and the mother because one of her sons was safe.

"My turn, my turn!" Daniel cried.

The scene was repeated.

She made them stand in separate corners in the parlor while she and Mrs. Barnes pulled the mattress upstairs again.

"Thank you for your help. I don't know what I would have done without you, Mrs. Barnes."

Still trembling, Maribel sat down at the kitchen table and took deep breaths. What had they been thinking? They could have been crippled or killed!

"How long do we have to stay here, Mum?" Daniel asked.

"Maybe the rest of the afternoon! I'm so angry! Wait 'til your father comes home!"

Frank Todd strolled down the street, whistling and swinging his newspaper. He came in the front door, expecting his family to rush to him as they usually did. Instead he found his two oldest standing in opposite corners of the parlor, their faces to the walls, and Gregory sitting on the bottom step fighting back tears.

"What's the matter?" he asked, drawing the boy onto his lap.

"You're gonna spank Wicky and Daniel."

"Now why would I do that?"

Maribel came from the kitchen, wiping her hands on her apron.

"Get over here and tell your father what you've done," she said to the two boys.

They walked slowly to their father's chair.

"Well?" Frank asked.

"We climbed up on the roof."

"Whatever for?"

"To see if the chimney was big enough for Santa Claus."

Frank brought his hand up to his mouth to hide a smile.

"And how did you get down?"

"We jumped! Mum caught us. She was standing on a mattress, and we knocked her over!" They giggled.

"Go back to the corner now. I'll deal with you in a minute."

He guided Maribel into the kitchen. She moved into the circle of his arms and began to sob.

"Oh, Frank, I was so scared! And I didn't know where you were working. I didn't know what to do."

She told him about Mrs. Barnes and the mattress.

He hugged her. "I'm so proud of you! Such a good idea."

He went back into the parlor, snapping his fingers to indicate that the boys were to stand in front of him.

"Now, what shall I do with you? Put a sign on the roof telling Santa Claus to skip our house?"

"No, Papa, please don't!"

"Maybe I should spank you."

Ricky and Daniel looked down at their shoes and mumbled.

"Well, you're lucky. When I was a boy my papa never spanked us on Christmas Eve, so I won't either. But you are never, never to climb up on the roof again, do you understand? Now, go to your room, all of you, and stay there 'til suppertime."

Shortly after six the relatives began to arrive. Frank's mother and father, his two brothers who were also his partners in the construction business, their wives, and five more children. Maribel filled the dining room table with the roast and potatoes and corn out of tins. The other women had brought cakes and pies and puddings.

The conversation among the children centered on

what Santa Claus was going to bring them, and among the adults it was the railroad, which would soon come to San Diego. The construction business could only get better; they would be hiring more workers in the spring after the rainy season. Maribel happily reflected that her parents would be able to visit them.

When the grandfather clock in the hall chimed eight, the three boys began to worry. Everyone knew that Santa Claus came only when children were asleep and houses were dark. When were these people going home?

At first they were subtle, pretending to yawn, looking at the clock. Then Ricky came right out and asked when they were going to leave.

"Oh, it's early yet," Uncle Tony said with a smile.

They stayed.

The youngest cousins began to fall asleep on chairs and sofas.

"Doesn't matter for them," Daniel grumbled. "If Santa Claus goes to their house, it'll be dark and he'll think they're asleep and leave 'em presents. But he's gonna pass us up!"

The adults were amused by the boys' obvious frustration.

Uncle William got up and walked to the window. "Oh, what do I see?" he asked.

The three boys looked at one another in horror. Daniel grabbed coats and threw them at his relatives. Ricky blew out candles, and Gregory ran to the stairs, climbing as fast as he could and stubbing his toe in the process. All three were in tears.

"Now, Boys," their mother said soothingly, "It's not Santa Claus, not yet. Uncle William made a mistake. But it is time for everyone to go home and get ready for bed."

Later Frank and Maribel stood in the doorway to the nursery and looked at the three, bundled under the covers and sleeping soundly. Gregory with his thumb in his mouth, Daniel with his two hands pressed together as though he had fallen asleep while praying, Ricky twisting his hair in his fingers.

"They look so angelic, don't they?" she whispered.

"Come on, Dear, let's get to bed. Tomorrow will be another eventful day."

The Magic Shirts

1890

"He who ack…acknowledges me before men will I ack…acknowledge before My Father in Heaven. Matthew 10:32"

The priest smiled at the Indian girl's efforts. "Excellent, Mary, excellent. Do you know what the word 'acknowledge' means?"

"Yes, Father. It means to see something and to know what it is."

"Yes. Another word for it is 'recognize'. You're reading very well. Soon you will be able to help me teach the others to read. Would you like that?"

"Oh, yes, Father, I would."

Mary Silver Star was twenty years old that winter. Until the previous summer she had been known only as Silver Star, her Lakota name, but after her Christian baptism she had taken the name Mary.

Their entire village had been moved to the Pine Ridge Agency in 1885. Once she had shared a warm tipi with her family, but now she lived with five other women in a wooden hut that did little to keep out the cold. Her two older brothers, Runs Like The Wind and Lame Deer, didn't like the restricted life and ran away to join Sitting Bull two years earlier. Her parents both died of a measles epidemic the previous winter. So perhaps it was natural that the young woman would seek solace in the new religion.

The priest, Father Andrew McCormack, had been born in County Cork and ordained in Boston. The Indians were amused by his red hair, the color of fire, and his freckles, for which they had no analogy, but he had earned their respect. He had seen Silver Star's potential as a teacher for her people, and he tried hard to get her to read the Bible and to accept Christianity.

On a cold, cloudless day in early December, Mary's two brothers rode into the village. She hadn't seen them since shortly after their parents' deaths, and she ran to them excitedly.

"I'm so happy to see you!"

"Silver Star, you're wearing the dress of the whites."

Lame Deer didn't like the long woolen dress with full sleeves she wore instead of her buckskin dress of years past. "Are you eating well?" He looked at the other Indians in the settlement and remarked that everyone looked gaunt.

Runs Like The Wind said scornfully, "The whites were going to take care of our every need if we came to the reservation. Look at the people! When was the last time you had meat, Silver Star?"

"Oh, let's not talk of that," she begged. "What are you doing here?"

Father McCormack approached. "Are these your brothers, Mary? Will you introduce me?"

When the two men and their sister were alone, Lame Deer asked, "What was it he called you, Silver Star? Mary? Where did that come from?"

"Mary is my Christian name."

"Surely you haven't taken the white man's religion?"

"As a matter of fact, I have."

"But why? How could you?"

She sat down before her brothers and spoke in a quiet voice.

"Ever since I was a little child, I have believed in the Great Spirit, the Creator, the Protector. If I were troubled, I would go off to a quiet place and I would ask the Great Spirit to help me. I was so alone after our father and our mother died. You were not here. The priest became my friend.

"He taught me to speak the language of the whites and to read the Bible. It is a curious thing, these marks on paper. The whites set great store by it. They do not seem to realize that the paper can fall into a stream or into a fire and the marks on the paper can disappear. But the stories we learned as children will live forever if we pass them on. We Lakota will pass our knowledge of the Great Spirit from generation to generation through words and songs."

"So if it can be destroyed, this Bible, what good is it?" Lame Deer asked.

"It is an interesting book of stories," she said. "It tells about the Great Spirit, only they call him God, and how He created the land and the water and the sky. How he created First Man and his woman and all the creatures. The stories are similar to those we have learned and so they must be true.

"And soon there will be a celebration of the birth of the son of the Great Spirit, Jesus Christ. He became a human being in order to teach the people how to live to please His Father."

Runs Like The Wind asked, "And what does he look like, this Jesus Christ?"

Mary went to the box near her sleeping robe and very carefully removed a picture, which she handed to her oldest brother.

He sneered, "Just as I thought! A white man! How do you explain that?"

Mary considered it for a moment and then said, "Well, he lived far away, in another place where the

Lakota do not live. That is why he doesn't look like us."

"Convenient, Silver Star, very convenient."

She continued, "The men with the black faces, the ones we call the buffalo soldiers, He doesn't look like them either. And yet many of them believe that He is Son of the Great Spirit."

"And where does he live, this son of the Great Spirit?"

"He is dead. He died many, many moons ago. Crucified."

"What does that mean, crucified?"

Mary drew a cross in the dirt floor, then showed the position in which Christ died. Explaining the nails was difficult, for the Lakota fastened with leather thongs.

"And you have accepted this new religion? Truly? What do you have to do now?"

Mary answered, "Believe that Jesus is the Son of the Great Spirit, that he lived as a human being, and that he was crucified for us."

"What does that mean?"

"I'm not quite sure I understand it all. The priest teaches us that human beings are basically, well not exactly bad, but unworthy of going to Heaven, which is what they call the Happy Hunting Grounds. Somehow, when Jesus died and lived again, it made all people worthy."

Runs Like The Wind smiled. "Well, now we're getting somewhere! Silver Star, have you heard of Wovoka?"

"The holy man of the Paiutes? Yes, I have heard."

Her brother was clearly excited. "He teaches that if

we are good, don't steal or tell untruths, then there will be a great upheaval of the earth and the white men will all disappear. And more than that! All of the warriors who are dead will come back to life after three days, and the buffalo herds will come back, too! And to make ourselves worthy we must dance the Ghost Dance."

"But how can that be?" Mary asked. "Only Jesus can live again. No other human being can do this on earth, only in Heaven, and only if they believe in Jesus as the Son of the Great Spirit."

"That's the white man's teaching again. Don't believe it. Anyway, we've come to ask you to make us Ghost Dance shirts. We need them to dance in and because they will keep us safe from the white man's bullets."

"But I don't know how to make shirts that will protect you from bullets!"

Lame Deer explained, "It's the symbols that are painted on them that are magic. Just make us the shirts. We will paint the symbols."

"But I don't have any cloth."

Lame Deer unwrapped his blanket and handed her pale blue cloth, enough for shirts for both brothers. Mary didn't want to ask where it had come from.

"So," he asked, "will you make the shirts for us?"

"Yes," she said.

Mary had serious misgivings about this thing she had agreed to do. She didn't believe that any shirts, no matter what kind of painting, would protect her brothers from the white man's bullets. And it went against her new beliefs. Then, too, if Father McCormack found out about it, he would be very unhappy. Perhaps he wouldn't let her teach the children to read.

She decided that she could not lie about what she was doing, but she would be very careful so the priest wouldn't find out. If he asked her, perhaps she could answer in a way that would not be a lie and yet would not tell all the truth. This, she decided, would be acceptable.

As it happened, the priest did see her working on the cloth and asked what she was making. She was genuinely unnerved by his question, and he assumed she was making a Christmas present, so he said no more.

At last, after more than a week, the shirts were finished.

Mary had told her brothers to meet her in a clearing away from the village. Looking around nervously to be sure they weren't being observed, she removed the blue shirts from under her blanket.

"They're beautiful, Silver Star," Lame Deer said.

"Yes, they are good," Runs Like The Wind agreed.

"So what happens now?" the girl asked. "How will you paint them?"

"With bark and walnut shells."

"No, I mean, what kind of pictures will you paint?"

"Sun and moons, crescent moons as well as full moons, and stars, and, I think, hawks," Lame Deer said.

"Careful, Brother," Runs Like The Wind cautioned, "you must not tell too much."

"But Silver Star is our sister. Our little sister."

"Yes, but she also considers the white man priest her friend. She said so."

Mary lowered her head. It made her sad and uncomfortable to realize that her older brother didn't trust her. Lame Deer hugged her and whispered, "Our brother is always too cautious, Silver Star. He distrusts the whites, more than I do. Don't be hurt by what he says."

The two young men drew their sister into their embrace and thanked her again for the shirts. They mounted their horses.

Runs Like The Wind raised his hand in farewell. "Silver Star, when we see you again, it will all be over! The new time will be here, the warriors and our parents will live again, and the whites will all be gone."

"Be careful," she called.

Runs Like The Wind laughed, "We don't have to be careful. We have the magic shirts."

She ran after them. "Where are you going now?"

"To Wounded Knee Creek."

At the Mass on Christmas Eve Father McCormack allowed Mary to read the story from the second chapter of Luke. She had practiced it over and over and was able to read clearly, with no mistakes. As she finished, she looked for his approval and saw him smile.

One of the men had killed a deer, and so everyone had a little meat for their Christmas feast. The priest tried to teach them some Christmas carols, and, though the people didn't want to sing, they liked to listen to his husky voice.

On the fourth day after Christmas, as Mary was reading from the Bible to some of the children, she heard shouting outside and then wails. She ran into the clearing. The priest was shouting instructions to some of the women, telling them to bring blankets to his wagon.

"Father, what is it? What's wrong?" she asked.

He was short of breath as he hitched the horses. "Trouble! At Big Foot's Camp. The Army. Guns. Many people killed."

"But why?"

"I don't know. Probably something to do with the Ghost Dance."

Mary felt a pain in her chest as she whispered, "Where?"

"Wounded Knee Creek."

"Father, you've got to take me with you! Please!"

"No, Mary, it's no place for you. You stay here."

"I can help you, Father."

"No."

"Father, please! My brothers…my brothers went to Wounded Knee Creek."

He looked at her face streaked with tears and her quivering lower lip.

"Get in. Maybe you'll be able to help after all."

It was eighteen long miles to Wounded Knee Creek.

Mary rode in silence, shivering despite her woolen shawl. Father MacCormack turned and grabbed one of the blankets from the wagon. She took it and wrapped it around them both. The sky was gray, the clouds low and ominous, the wind gusty. The shallow stream they had just crossed was frozen.

"A blizzard is coming, for sure," the priest said.

Occasionally he looked over and saw her lips

moving in prayer. He said little; he wouldn't have known what to say.

The priest didn't approve of the Ghost Dance or Wovoka's prophecies. They were against everything he believed, and, as a white man, he feared their prediction that all whites would be destroyed. But, on the other hand, he had great sympathy for these people. He worked in conjunction with the government but didn't approve of its actions. The government had repeatedly cut food rations. After all, it was believed, wouldn't a hungry Indian become a better farmer? No matter that the soil on the reservation was poor and the rainfall insufficient.

Father MacCormack and the girl strained to see as they approached the creek. There were soldiers everywhere, wagons, fires. And bodies. So many bodies.

The priest got down from the wagon and extended his hand to Mary. An Army officer approached and demanded to know why they had come.

"I'm Father McCormack from Pine Ridge. I thought perhaps I could help. I have some medical training. Our doctor was out of the village, but I sent someone to find him and bring him here."

"And her?" the officer asked, pointing at Mary.

"She's my helper."

The officer growled, "Just don't get in the way."

Father McCormack and Mary walked among the dead and injured. There were so few who could be helped. There were tears in the priest's eyes as he muttered, "Oh, God, no! Women! Children! Babies!"

Mary shivered as she saw a patch of pale blue ahead on the ground. She ran to it, then stopped beside

Runs Like the Wind, his hands clutching a rifle and his blue shirt red with blood. His eyes were open but sightless.

The priest came up behind her and put his hand on her shoulder. She stood there, not crying or screaming, just staring at her brother.

Finally, she spoke. "I must find Lame Deer."

But nowhere could she see another pale blue shirt. She ran back to the officer they had met minutes before.

"Please," she begged, "where are the others? There must be others!"

The man looked at her with disdain and walked away. She began to cry. A soldier approached and whispered, "They're not all dead. Some of 'em have been taken prisoner. Over there."

Mary ran in the direction indicated. Four men, one of them her brother, were in a wagon guarded by a dozen soldiers. As she approached, she could see chains around the ankles of the Indians. She breathed a sign of relief as she noted that the blue shirt bore no blood stains.

Surprisingly, none of the soldiers resisted her efforts to push forward to the wagon.

"Lame Deer," she whispered. No response, so she again said his name.

He lifted his head and looked into her eyes. It took several seconds for him to realize who she was.

"Silver Star."

"Yes. Are you all right? Are you all right?" she asked.

"What happened? The Dance…the Dance…we danced just the way Wovoka told us to. And the shirts…they were supposed to protect us." He looked down at his chest, at the pictures of sun and moons and stars and hawks, then shook his head in disbelief.

Father McCormack finally caught up with Mary.

"What will happen to these men?" he asked a guard.

"Prison."

Mary began to cry.

"It's too bad about the shirt," the priest said to himself. "If he weren't wearing the shirt, I could perhaps say that he was one of my Lakota who came to stop his brother." He lifted his eyes to heaven and whispered, "Lord, forgive me for being willing to lie. But maybe two wrongs do sometimes make a right. Perhaps I could have saved his soul through a lie. Oh, Lord, give me a way to help him."

The priest and the girl were pushed out of the way as the wagon began to move.

"Come, Mary, we have to see if we can help any of the others. Don't cry. I have to think. Perhaps there will be a way to save your brother."

On a cold, cloudless afternoon in January 1894, Father McCormack headed for his cabin and the steaming teakettle.

Yes, he was still at Pine Ridge. He had an opportunity to be sent to another church. Two doctors had said that if he were to have a change of scenery, the nightmares might stop. He had seriously considered it, had prayed about it, but in the end he knew that he must stay. Someone else would have come to take his place, someone who hadn't been at Wounded Knee that day, who didn't know how the

Lakota had suffered.

To make sure that people back East heard the truth about the "battle" in which women and children victims outnumbered the men two to one, Father MacCormack relied on his memories and his family connections. A magazine had published his article about Wounded Knee, and that led to two others in which he described his life among the Lakota.

Those family connections had served Mary and Lame Deer as well. In the spring of 1891 Father McCormack had learned that the government was considering parole for some of the imprisoned Indian warriors on the condition that they join Buffalo Bill's traveling show. A revolutionary idea and one which generated a lot of controversy, but, in the end, it was implemented.

Without mentioning a word to Mary, the priest had written about Lame Deer to his cousin John, who was secretary to a congressman. Mary's brother had been an obedient prisoner and thus eligible for parole.

What Father McCormack had not foreseen was that his act of compassion would cost him the best teacher he had at Pine Ridge. Mary joined Buffalo Bill's troupe, too, and they traveled all over the country. She was faithful about writing the priest letters which he read over and over and which he shared with his Indians.

Pouring a cup of tea, he took from his pocket the letter that had just arrived that day. He marveled at the postmark, London!

Dear Father,

Can you believe it? We are in England. The language they speak here is English, yet I must try hard to understand them. There are many large stone buildings they call castles (I had to ask someone how to spell that word) and inside are rooms large enough for our whole village to be at the same time.

The people enjoy our show. They are (here is another new word) enthusiastic. I like that word. It is said that members of the Queen's family will come to our show soon.

I am writing to tell you wonderful news. You remember that I was teaching Lame Deer to read the Bible. He is a good student. He is enthusiastic. Yesterday he was baptized. It was the happiest day of my life.

I hope you are well, Father, and all the others, too. I will write again soon.

Mary

A Branch with No Twigs

1911

Dr. May Williams finally fell in love at the age of 39. It was the same year that her twin became a grandmother.

They were fraternal rather than identical twins.

Eliza took after their mother. Petite with strawberry-blonde hair, cornflower blue eyes, curves in all the right places. She was flirtatious, a good listener, and proficient in all the womanly arts like cooking and sewing. Eliza wanted nothing more than to marry young and have a family. She married the son of the richest man in town and produced their first child two days after their first anniversary.

May took after their father, whom she always called “Pops”. Two inches taller than Eliza, she had light brown hair which refused to curl, and she was as flat as the proverbial board. She might have been called plain until she smiled, revealing teeth that were beautiful and straight. But it was in her eyes that the magic lay. They were neither green nor brown nor gold but a combination of all three, and when she smiled those eyes sparkled and illuminated her face until one almost forgot that Eliza was considered the pretty sister.

Their mother despaired over May. While little Eliza played with dolls, May went with her father on his rounds, visiting his patients, helping him keep his medical records. She spent hour after hour in the clinic attached to their home.

The summer of Eliza’s wedding preceded May’s going away to Bryn Mawr. Eliza and Mother had been thrilled when the groom’s cousin from Chicago fell in love with May and disappointed when May told him that nothing would deter her from finishing her two years at Bryn Mawr and then going to the Women's Medical College of Pennsylvania. Practicing with Pops would be her dream come true.

When May came home to Binghamton after graduation, Eliza and Mother had been determined to find her a husband. They were constantly inviting eligible young men, and later not-so-young men, to dinner. May was always polite, even mildly interested, but many of these dinners were interrupted by medical emergencies, and it was clear where her priorities lay. Finally, when the twins turned thirty, Eliza and Mother gave up their matchmaking, convinced that May would never marry.

After Mother died in 1907, May and her father employed a housekeeper and continued to work in their clinic. May was busy and yet vaguely discontented. It wasn't something she could put into words until one of Eliza's sons developed an interest in genealogy.

"See here, this branch of the family tree is your grandfather, Josiah Williams, the one who died at the second battle of Bull Run. And here are his children, Grandpa Matthew and his brothers Mark and Luke. You can see how the branches divide into smaller branches and then twigs. Here's Mother and me and Catherine and Richard."

"Where am I on this tree, Joel?" May asked.

"Right here, next to Mother, this branch that doesn't have any twigs."

A branch with no twigs, she thought. By the time Joel has grandchildren, they probably won't remember anything about me. Unless I make some remarkable medical discovery, but that seems unlikely. What have

I done with my life? I've been so consumed with medicine that I didn't allow any time for a family, for a personal life. Even Pops managed to do that.

However, she wasn't able to do anything about this deficit in her life. Shortly after her conversation with her nephew, she began to notice changes in her father's behavior, such as his occasional inappropriate use of words. One evening, as they sat at the dinner table, he pointed at the bread and asked her to pass the stethoscope. On another occasion he became agitated when he couldn't find his notes for an anatomy exam the next day, an exam that he had taken nearly forty years earlier.

Alarmed, she began scanning his medical records as she filed them, praying that she wouldn't find a misdiagnosis or the wrong medication administered. She wondered what she would do if she were to find such a mistake. He wouldn't be able to continue in their practice and yet it would kill him. What was she going to do?

He broke his leg in December 1910. He had been standing on a stepladder to reach a box of Christmas ornaments and lost his balance.

The trauma of the fall seemed to escalate his dementia.

"You and I have something in common," he said to her one evening. "We both survived our spouses." She protested that she had never been married, and he seemed confused.

Sometimes in the morning, when she asked how he had slept, he described walks he had taken all night long.

He asked for his wife, wondering when she was

coming back, and he often called May by her mother's name.

He fretted over lost things, homework for a class, a non-existent book. He directed May to check closets where there were no closets, and he constantly worried that an intruder had taken the "lost" things. She wasn't sure what to say. Should she mollify him with something like, "Don't worry, I've put it away in a safe place" or try to explain the truth?

He attempted to get out of bed, and she worried constantly that he would fall and break his hip or neck. She didn't like tying his sheets to keep him in bed, but it was the only way for both of them to get any sleep.

His incontinence bothered her most. She had changed diapers on Eliza's children, but somehow the idea of changing a diaper on her father was too much. For years they had had Mrs. Perkins come in for half days, cleaning and cooking the noon meal. But her own family obligations made extended hours impossible. May hired a nurse to stay in the house and to take care of him while she saw patients.

One day while the nurse was out for a walk, while May read and thought her father was asleep, he took his diaper off and soiled the bed. The nurse soon came back and proceeded to clean and change him. Kindly she asked what had happened, and he pointed a finger at May and said, "She stole my underwear and threw it away!"

He would rediscover words and use them over and over, sometimes in sentences that would leave May giggling. It reminded her of Eliza's children when they learned to talk. One day the new word was "nervous". She couldn't help but laugh. His voice shook slightly as he sang, "Jesus, Jesus, don't be nervous..."

"So how is your latest love affair going?" he asked her.

"Do you know who I am?" she whispered.

"Why, you're Mrs. Turnip."

"And who am I supposed to be having this love affair with?"

He sighed. "Why, Mr. Turnip, of course!"

One day, May came back from house calls to find him sitting up in bed, looking very much like his old self. She took the mashed potatoes and chicken from the nurse and began to feed him herself. He repeatedly wiped his mouth on the blanket instead of the towel, and she told him several times not to. He winked at her and said in a voice loud enough for Mrs. Perkins to hear, "She doesn't have enough laundry to do."

He asked if his wife knew where he was, and May explained that she had died many years earlier. "I know about Dorothy," he said, "but didn't I marry someone else later on?"

He was a chatterbox that afternoon, and May reluctantly tore herself away to start office hours.

It was the last day he was fully awake.

May watched as the nurse fed Pops. Unable to chew, he had already been moved to soft foods. The nurse put a spoonful of oatmeal into his mouth, but it ran out. She spooned milk into him and gently held his mouth closed while she told him to swallow. When she removed her hand, the milk oozed out onto his chin.

The next day he was completely unresponsive. His eyes were closed; he seemed unaware of May's presence. She tried shouting, clapping her hands, washing his face with a washcloth wrung out in cold water. She sat beside him, holding his hand and stroking his hair. "I love you, Pops," she whispered, "and I want you back again, the way things were. What would I do without you?"

Those last days were very difficult for May. His major organs—lungs, heart, liver, kidneys—were shutting down. She was awake much of every night. She would sleep for a couple of hours, then something, usually a nightmare, would wake her, and she would quietly go into his room, being careful not to disturb the nurse in the adjoining bedroom. May would stare at him, willing him to wake long enough to say something to her, one final bit of wisdom, one final acknowledgement that she had been important to him.

One evening she finished her office hours a little after eight o'clock. She went to the kitchen and made a cup of tea and took it into her father's bedroom, where he had slept without waking for thirteen days. Those little visits had become a habit, but she never stayed more than a few minutes, just long enough to stroke his hair and whisper her love.

His eyes were open.

The nurse told her that he had been like that for about twenty minutes but he couldn't speak.

May moved her head to see if his eyes would follow, and they did.

Excitedly, she sat down, took his hand, and began a flood of conversation.

"Pops, if you can understand me, close your eyes and keep them shut long enough that I'll know it's not just a blink."

Oh, how he tried! The eyelids fluttered for a full minute, then closed completely, squeezed shut. And then he cried, whether from frustration or relief, she didn't know.

"Are you in pain?" she asked. "I think that you probably are not because I've watched your face in sleep when we've changed your sheets and have moved the leg. But if you are in pain, Pops, I want you to close your eyes again. If you don't have pain, keep them open."

She sat for a long time, watching him. His eyes were wide open, staring at her. She breathed a sigh of relief, knowing that he wasn't suffering physically.

"Can you squeeze my hand?"

It nearly broke her heart to see him struggle so much, and in the end there was only slight pressure, nothing more. He seemed exhausted and soon drifted into sleep.

May sat with him for an hour and then went to the window. How beautiful the night is, she thought. Diamond stars scattered on a black velvet sky. She felt strangely content. She knew that Pops would never recover but was grateful for the opportunity to communicate with him, if only in a primitive way. There were things she wanted to ask him, notably whether he could hear her during those thirteen days. She would ask him the next day and then something else the following day. Not too much; she didn't want to overtire him.

The nurse woke May shortly after midnight to tell her that he was gone.

Four weeks after her father's death, May was going

through the motions of seeing her patients during the day while at night suffering from insomnia. She extended her evening office hours so that she was there from 5:30 to 8:30. Actually, it was often after 9 before she closed the clinic.

One Wednesday, she looked out into the waiting room at 8:30, hoping it would be empty, and saw George Ebbersten.

"I'm not here as a patient but as a friend," he said. "I can tell you haven't been sleeping. Dark circles under your eyes. And you look thin, like you haven't been eating well. I've been noticing you at church lately. You're suffering, I know. I thought you might need a friend to talk to."

May started to protest, but he said, "You and Doc were there for me when Flora died. Good friends. Let me help you now."

May locked the clinic, and they went into the house. She put the teakettle on the stove and a tin of shortbread on the table.

George was fifty-nine, tall, with deep blue eyes, white hair and trimmed beard and moustache. He and Flora had lived above their grocery store for twenty-six years. Three years earlier, after her sudden death from a stroke, he had suffered from many of the same symptoms which he now said he saw in May.

Pops had started inviting George to dinner at least once a week and had taught him to play chess. The three of them had passed many pleasant evenings together.

"Something smells good," George said.

"Oh, my dinner."

"At this hour?"

"The housekeeper left it warming in the oven, but I wasn't hungry." She sighed. "I usually have to throw it out."

"You have to eat, have to keep your strength up."

"I hate to eat alone. I hate being alone. This house is so quiet. Nothing but the ticking of the clock."

"I know what you mean," he said. "I would stay in the store long after closing, doing needless inventories, rearranging the shelves, anything to keep me from having to go upstairs to that silence. I guess that's why you spend so much time in the clinic."

She nodded.

"Why don't you get a dog?" he suggested.

"Oh, I couldn't go through that. A grown dog isn't bad, but those early months, the accidents on the rug, the chewed-up slippers...I saw what a problem it was when Eliza's children had a dog."

"Well, it was just a thought," he said.

On the following Sunday, George sat beside her in church. She was so grateful for the company that she invited him back to the house for lunch.

The next weekend he appeared at her door with a brown cocker spaniel.

"How beautiful!" she exclaimed. "Is he yours?"

"Actually, it's a she, and I was hoping you'd take her."

May looked at him quizzically.

"You know old Mr. Hansen died last week. Daisy is his dog, and I asked his children if I could give her to you. They really don't have room for another pet."

May knelt down and stroked Daisy's soft coat. The dog looked up at her with sad eyes.

"Oh, you poor thing. You're as miserable as I am." Turning to George, she whispered, "Thank you."

All summer George came to dinner at least twice a week. May told him that the housekeeper could cook just as easily for two as for one. After dinner, they played chess.

She found herself looking forward to those evenings. After their game they would take Daisy for a walk, and the exercise helped her to sleep better.

George often brought her little treats from the store. "You're still too thin," he teased.

On the Fourth of July he kissed her good night for the first time, and she had never known such happiness.

Eliza asked, "What's going on between you two? Everyone has noticed that you sit with him in church and that you spend so much time together."

"We're friends, nothing more," May replied, but even as she said it she knew it wasn't the truth.

As summer progressed into autumn, she found herself thinking about him more and more, wondering what it would be like to be loved by him, to be married to him. She longed to tell him how she felt but held back. She had seen how devoted he and Flora had been to each another, had always counted them among the happiest of married couples. What would it be like to be George's second wife? Would he constantly compare the two women? Could she live with a man who had been so happy with someone else? But then she had had so little real happiness, pride in her profession, yes, but not happiness. Wouldn't being his second wife be better than what she had now?

December 15 was George's sixtieth birthday. His sons and their families would come the following Sunday, so May invited him to dinner, only this time she planned to cook it herself. She posted a sign for two weeks that there would be no office hours on that date and that another doctor could be called in an emergency.

She made roast chicken and fried potatoes and a chocolate cake for dessert.

As she dressed, she studied her reflection in the mirror. Her face and figure had rounded with added pounds, but not unattractively. Her hair had turned prematurely white in a broad streak in the front, but it was pretty. On this night her cheeks were pink with excitement and her eyes twinkled.

She said to Daisy, "Mother would turn over in her grave if she knew what I plan to do, but I have to take the chance. Life is passing me by."

The dog barked her approval.

George arrived with a box of shortbread and a kiss. May poured two glasses of sherry, and they talked about current events, their families, the church, the weather. Everything but their relationship.

Dinner was perfect, and May beamed under George's praise. She made a pot of tea, and they sat down in front of the fireplace.

She moved closer to him, snuggling against his shoulder, trying through the power of her thoughts to get him to kiss her. And he did, twice, three times.

For the longest time the only sounds were the crackling of the fire and Daisy's snoring. May wondered if George could hear her heart pounding.

It was clear that he wasn't going to make a move.

It was up to her.

"Will you marry me?" she whispered.

"What?!"

She repeated it.

He abruptly stood up and faced the fire, his back to her and his hands on the mantle.

"I can't," he said.

She tried to remain calm. "Why not? Don't you care for me?" She didn't dare use the word "love", didn't want to scare him away.

"Of course I care. That's not the point."

"Then what is it, George?"

"I'm old enough to be your father."

She sighed in relief.

He continued, "And you know my heart isn't strong. I'm sure to die long before you, and I don't want you grieving over me."

She stood and wrapped her arms around his waist as he continued to stare into the fire, his back to her.

"George, we don't know what the future holds. Why deny ourselves happiness? If you were to die, I would grieve for you the rest of my life. Let me do it as your wife, not just a friend. I love you, and I thought maybe you loved me, too."

He turned and pressed her to his chest.

"I do, May, I love you."

"So, will you marry me?"

He laughed. "I'm old-fashioned, I guess. The man should do the proposing. Take it back, what you said."

"And if I do?"

"Then I'll ask you."

"I take it back, George."

The Empty Chair

1928

Mary Ivanovna looked at her family gathered around the table. Her husband Sergei, her daughters Olga and Varvara, who were twelve and thirteen, her sons Nicholas and Daniel, ages fourteen and sixteen. The samovar with hot tea bubbled in the corner of the kitchen, and the abundant breakfast attested to the prosperity of the past year.

They had just come from the Christmas church service. A long, long night by anyone's standards, but the *staroverii*, the Old Believers, were used to it. Six o'clock Christmas Eve until six o'clock Christmas morning. A break of twenty minutes every three hours. There were no chairs to sit on. At various points in the service each person had to stretch out flat on the floor, face down, forehead against the wooden slats in abject humility. But mostly they stood throughout the long, cold night. A difficult religion, this, and yet Mary drew comfort from it, especially thinking of their families back in the Old Country where the Communists had forbidden any practice of religion, any hint of God. How could one not believe in God? Mary felt reasonably sure that her brothers still believed and that her mother had gone to her death believing. Of course, their letters never mentioned it. It would be foolhardy to write about, and such a letter wouldn't get past the Soviet censors anyway. But what about the young, what about the children who would be brought up to believe that there is no God, that the State is the Supreme Being? What kind of life would they have, these children? What kind of country would Russia become?

Mary removed her scarf which, according to church rules, had covered her hair completely with no wisps of the graying blonde escaping. She brought eggs and ham and porridge to the table.

Sergei, father and ultimate authority in the home as Russian fathers always had been, was served first. As was the custom, he ate as much as he pleased, with the children and then Mary herself taking from what was left. He worked so hard to provide for them all that no one begrudged him this sign of respect. Sergei was a good man, and she loved him…now. She hadn't when she had arrived as a mail-order bride in 1910. It had taken awhile for her to get over her love and grief for Ivan, her first husband, who had died in an accident on the farm. Sergei was a good man; he never struck her (there's a blessing!) and he practiced the old religion faithfully.

She put a plate of black bread between her sons. They looked to their father, who smiled and indicated that they could start filling their plates. Both Nicholas and Daniel looked so much like Sergei…short, stocky and muscular, dark hair and blue eyes. Nicholas had a cleft in his chin, just like Mary's oldest brother Daniel, the one who had died in Poland in the Great War. Her sons would probably follow Sergei into the coal mines. A hard life, it was true, but good money for little education.

Varvara and Olga brought cups of strong tea to their father and brothers. Varvara, dark-haired and tall, was outspoken and had an opinion about everything. Olga, blonde like her mother, was quiet, more domestic. Mary sometimes thought that they should have been named Martha and Mary, like the sisters of Lazarus in the Bible, but a child was always named for the saint on whose day he or she had been born.

The conversation grew more animated and louder. Mary sliced cake at the counter, then turned to place it on the table. Her eyes fell on the empty chair—her own, of course—and suddenly she felt breathless and in pain. Because there really was an empty chair, not just her own. There was another who should have been there.

Her daughter Anna. The daughter she had left behind in Russia.

Mary had been bride and mother and widow within the space of less than two years. Her brothers had arranged this marriage to Sergei, who had gone from a neighboring village to Pennsylvania in America, made some money, and then asked his family to find him a wife. It had never occurred to her to resist the marriage, barely a year after Ivan's death. Women in Russia went through life being told what to do by a man, first father, brothers when the father died, then husband.

But Anna was one year old and sickly.

"Go to America, Mary," her own mother had said. "Next year when the little one is stronger I will bring her to you."

But the next year Mary's mother had written that Anna was still too frail to make the trip. The following year the problem had been money. As the years passed, it was always something. The Great War. The Revolution. Danger. What if something happened to Anna on the way to America?

Mary had written faithfully, at least twice a month. Tender letters to her little girl, comforting her and promising that soon, soon they would be together again.

The letters from Mary's mother changed. She no longer mentioned bringing Anna to America nor did she refer to Anna as Mary's daughter. The letters were filled with pride in Anna's accomplishments as she learned to read and write, as she excelled in school, as she learned to sew.

Slowly, painfully, Mary came to the realization that Anna would never come, that Mary's own mother had taken over the role of mother.

"How could she do it?" Mary had cried as she lay in Sergei's arms at night.

"I think I can understand," he said. "Not that it's right, of course not. But she has no other daughter now. You were the only one. Your brothers are there, but that's different. A woman needs a daughter, and she has taken yours."

Mary had cried night after night, so much that she miscarried what would have been her sixth child. Sergei had watched helplessly as she suffered.

"I know it's little consolation," he had said, "but you have to admit that your mother loves Anna…"

"It's not love, it's obsession!"

"At any rate, she will always care for her, always be there for her. Please, Sweetheart, you must try to pull yourself together. You're scaring me! You're so pale and thin. I don't want to lose you."

Mary and Sergei had no way of knowing how close they had come to getting Anna back. Daniel, her oldest brother and the one she loved best, had been the first to realize that his mother would never take Anna to America. He had argued with her in his role as head of the fatherless family.

"I'm your mother, Daniel. How can you break my

heart like this?"

When that didn't work, she tried appealing to his sense of fairness. "Mary has two other daughters now. Without Anna I would have nothing."

Out of loyalty to his mother, Daniel didn't write to Mary that Anna was never allowed to see Mary's letters, nor that Mary's name was never mentioned around the little girl, nor that the child called her grandmother "Mama". But he did come to a decision and announced it on one of his leaves from the Army.

"As soon as the war is over, I'm taking her to America. That's it! That's final! Do you understand, Mama?"

But when the war was over, when the men came back, Daniel remained in a shallow grave somewhere in Poland, and his pledge regarding Anna was buried with him.

Still sitting around the table, the family began to sing Christmas songs.

Mary walked into her bedroom and closed the door. Opening the drawer with her underclothes, she pulled out a piece of gray paper. She could recite it from memory now, and she wondered briefly why she kept re-reading it when each time was like a knife cutting into her heart. The words were in Russian, a beautiful script.

Dear Mary,

You will notice that I don't write 'Dear Mother'. As far as I am concerned, you are not my mother. You are nothing to me, nothing.

I am getting married in the Spring. His name is Yuri Denisovich Pavlov, and he is a teacher in the school in the town. I shall continue to work as a seamstress, even after we have children.

It is time for you to stop writing to me. Nothing will change, ever! You think you can abandon me and go running off to America, forget about me for years while you have other children, and then expect me to forgive you? Stop those lies about Mama keeping your letters from me, about how she supposedly persuaded you to leave me 'til I got stronger and could make the journey. Mama told me the truth. I believe her, and I don't believe you. I am thankful that she loved me enough to take your place in my life, otherwise I would have suffered greatly. Even though she was my grandmother, I shall always think of her as Mama because she was the only mother I have known.

Do not write to me ever again. I tell you now that I will burn your letters without reading them.
Anna Ivanovna

The door to the bedroom opened slowly, and Sergei came to her. Tilting her chin upward, he gently brushed away the tears on her cheeks. Wordlessly, he held her close as her shoulders convulsed in sorrow.

"Sweetheart, I know, I know. But you have four other children who love you and need you. And I need you. Why don't you burn the letter? Come, the children want to sing your favorite song for you.

Come."

"In a minute," she whispered. He left the room, and she folded the letter.

She tucked it back into the drawer. Despite the pain of those words, she wasn't ready to destroy her last link to Anna.

The Housekeeper

1943

In 1934, sixteen-year old Mary Rose Urbancic went to work as a governess for the Weinstein family in the elegant Squirrel Hill section of Pittsburgh. It wasn't at all strange that she, though barely five feet tall and one hundred pounds, could take on the responsibility of three children because she herself was the fourth oldest of nine. Like her two older sisters, Mary Rose had left school to enter domestic service. One less mouth to feed at home, and another salary coming in.

How the Weinstein children loved her stories! It was inconceivable to them that the huge family lived in a house with just three bedrooms. One for Mama and Papa, one for all the girls, the last for all the boys. All the children had chores to do, even before going to school in the morning. The boys chopped wood, the girls fed the chickens and gathered berries. They walked almost two miles to school. Mary Rose described the house in great detail and, when asked where the toilet was, replied, "Outside". Mama had been known to give birth in the morning and milk the cow at sunset. And, unlike city dwellers who had electric lights, country folk like the Urbancics went to bed soon after dark, using candles to light their way.

Over the years the Catholic Mary Rose and the Jewish Weinsteins had learned much about each other. Mary Rose would sing Christmas carols to the children at night, and she took part in their Passover, Rosh Hashana, and Hanukkah.

When the war started, the gardener and the chauffeur enlisted, and the cook and housekeeper went to work in the factories. Mr. Weinstein could drive himself to work or take the bus, and the children could learn to garden, but what about the house? what about the cooking?

"I can do it, Mrs. Weinstein," Mary Rose had said.

"All the cooking and cleaning? No, no, it's just too much, Mary Rose."

"But our meals can be much simpler; actually with the rationing they'll have to be. And now that the children are growing, the house doesn't get as messy."

It was true. Sarah was eighteen and at the university. Nathan was fourteen, and Miriam was already twelve.

So for the past two years Mary Rose had kept the house running smoothly and their stomachs full.

Six months ago she met Pete Kowalski at church. He was the cousin of Alice, her best friend in the city and housekeeper for the Waldbaums in the next block. Pete was a coal miner and therefore had a deferment. At least once a month Pete would try to enlist, but the answer was always the same. He was needed more at home.

"I feel like I should wear my mining helmet out on the street," he said. "People stare at me and I know they're wondering why an able-bodied man isn't off fighting."

And he was able-bodied. Broad and muscular, with curly hair even darker brown than her own and the bluest eyes she had ever seen. She was too practical to believe in love at first sight, but this was darn close.

He told her he loved her two months after they met, and within a month after that they were talking about marriage. Whirlwind courtships were common during the war. Some couples had been known to meet on Friday and marry on Sunday, and then the husband shipped out on Tuesday.

The problem was that Pete worked in a mine outside the city, about an hour by train. If they married, when they married, Mary Rose would have to quit her job.

On one of her visits home, she confided in her sister Matilda.

"It's not that I don't love him; I do. But if I quit work now, Mama and Papa wouldn't have my salary coming in, and it's hard enough to make ends meet."

"And?"

"And I hate to leave the Weinsteins without a housekeeper. It's so hard to find one."

"How about if I take your job, Mary Rose? Think they'd hire me?"

"You? I thought you loved your job in the factory."

"I'm getting a bit tired of it, especially working the night shift. I'm ready for a change. The factory can get someone else for my job. So what do you think? Would they hire me?"

"Sure," Mary Rose said, her eyes twinkling, "especially if you came on my recommendation."

Any hesitation Mary Rose felt was dispelled by two events in November. On the tenth Pete's widowed mother died, and the next week the Urbancics received word that Joseph, eldest of the nine, was a prisoner of war. Suddenly life itself seemed fragile. Suddenly it seemed important to reach out and grab whatever happiness could be had, before it vanished.

So Mary Rose Urbancic made plans to marry Pete Kowalski on December 26, 1943, in the tiny church in which she had been baptized and confirmed.

The Weinsteins told Mary Rose to go up into the

attic and to take whatever furniture she and Pete could use.

"We don't need much, Mrs. Weinstein. Pete's house is pretty well furnished."

"But it might be fun for you to have something that you bring to the house, Mary Rose."

The attic was dusty and dark, but there were treasures there. She found two lovely hurricane lamps. A footstool with a compartment beneath the faded tapestry cushion would be perfect for sewing supplies. And in the corner was a desk, actually what was called a secretary. She laughed when Mrs. Weinstein told her that it was a reproduction of a Chinese Chippendale. What a funny name! There was a slanted panel that could be pulled down to write on and above it were three shelves for books. Standing on the floor next to the secretary was the door that had concealed the shelves; it had come off its hinges. But the most extraordinary thing about the desk was the color, a bright orange with greenish-blue trim.

"I know it's bright," she wrote to Pete, "but I love orange. Can we take it, please?"

Now Pete was a practical man, and it tickled him to think that Mary Rose, whom he had always imagined to be just as practical, wanted to bring an orange desk into the house his mother had decorated in dark tones "so as not to show the dirt". He wasn't sure how the desk would look in the house, but he couldn't deny her this little pleasure. He promised to repair the unhinged door.

As the early days of December passed more and more quickly, Mary Rose became jittery. This three-story stone house had been her home for nearly ten years. Matilda came on the tenth to share her room and to be taught how to care for the Weinsteins. Mary Rose showed her sister how to make kasha knishes and matzo ball soup and wrote down instructions for corning beef, for surely with the end of the war would come restored abundance.

And then it was her last night in the house. They wouldn't hear of her cooking, they said, so Matilda and Sarah and Miriam and even Mrs. Weinstein had prepared a wonderful meal. They invited Pete to come, too, and to sleep in Nathan's room that night. In the morning, in a borrowed truck, Pete would take Mary Rose away. Never again would she enter this house as one of the family.

They sat around the dining room table. The five Weinsteins, Pete, Mary Rose, and Matilda. Mary Rose remembered that when she had first come, she and the children had eaten all but holiday meals in the kitchen. But when she alone remained of all the servants, the Weinsteins had insisted that she eat her meals with them.

Mr. Weinstein produced a bottle of fine claret, which he said had been saved for a special occasion, and he made a toast.

"To Mary Rose and Pete, happiness always. May Joseph be safe, and may the war be over soon."

The lump in her throat was so big that Mary Rose could hardly eat a bite.

About two o'clock in the morning, she woke. After tossing and turning for twenty minutes, she quietly got out of bed and went downstairs. She sat at the breakfast table and looked out over the back yard, now bathed in silver by the moon. She remembered playing there with the children when they were younger. Planting a garden, a victory garden, when the war began.

She vaguely remembered having been homesick when she first came, not strange because she had never been away from home before. But little by little this had become her home. She was a part of this family, as well as the family of her parents and brothers and sisters, and now Pete was going to be her family. Maybe that's what growing up means, she thought, becoming a part of other families.

A footstep on the stair. Mary Rose strained in the dim light to see who it was.

"Mrs. Weinstein," she said.

"What are you doing down here all alone at this hour?" the mother asked.

"Oh, I couldn't sleep."

"Nor could I." After a brief silence, she said, "You were so young when you first came here. You were so nervous during the interview that your knuckles were white. When I asked you the ages of your brothers and sisters, you had to stop and think."

"Oh, I remember that," Mary Rose said. "I was so overwhelmed by this house, all the silver and crystal and fine china. I was afraid that the children wouldn't like me, that you wouldn't like me. Tell me, why did you hire me? You must have interviewed other girls."

"Quite a few, actually."

"So, why me?"

"You were wearing a little wooden cross on a string."

"Joseph, my oldest brother, the one who...who's a P.O.W., he made one for each of us. But why did that make you hire me?"

"As you talked, you rubbed that little cross between your fingers, as though it were giving you courage and strength. I've always felt that way about my faith, that it gave me strength. Even though you were Catholic and I Jewish, I felt a bond between us.

"Mary Rose, you are almost like a daughter to me. I want you to be happy, really happy. I know Pete is proud, but if there is ever anything we can do for you, you will tell us, won't you? Promise you will."

Mary Rose was afraid to say a word, afraid that tears would start and never stop, so she just nodded.

The orange desk was the last thing to go into the truck.

"Well, that's all of it," Pete said. "Thank you for everything."

"You're welcome," Mr. Weinstein said. "You take good care of our girl here. Good-bye, my dear." He hugged Mary Rose.

Sarah, Nathan, and Miriam said tearful good-byes. Matilda promised to come home on the train on Christmas Eve.

"You understand why I can't come before then, don't you, Mary Rose? They need me."

Mrs. Weinstein stood off to the side. She handed Mary Rose a package. "The handkerchief is your something borrowed for the wedding. Since it's borrowed, you'll have to return it someday, and that'll be an excuse to come back. The other is your something old, the little silver heart pin that belonged to my aunt, and it's not to be returned. It's my gift to you. I want you to have it."

As the truck pulled away from the curb, Mary Rose began to cry. Pete patted her hand and said, "You'll see them again."

"I know, but it will never be the same."

He smiled. "Who's to say it won't be better?"

The Letter

1945

Mary Grace opened her eyes on Christmas morning and looked at her husband sleeping beside her. So often during the years of the war she had dreamed of this day. She had imagined that once he came home, everything would be perfect once again. And, yes, it was good, even wonderful, but not perfect.

Quietly, she slid out of bed, pulled on her pink bathrobe, and pulled the brush through her dark, curly hair. She went to the kitchen and started heating water for coffee. Outside the sky was gray, and it looked like it might snow. She sat down in the overstuffed chair next to the Christmas tree. Their first Christmas tree. Sam had shipped out just two months after their wedding nearly four years before, so she had spent that next Christmas and the others that followed with her family. She had promised herself that she wouldn't put up a tree in their apartment until he could be there with her to decorate it.

Last night, as they put her homemade ornaments on the little evergreen, her heart had been ready to burst with happiness. She had worried so much about him, afraid that he would be one of the many who didn't make it home. He had placed the gold foil angel on the top branch, had joined her in singing Christmas carols, had smiled at her memories of Christmases as a child. But when he didn't know she was looking, the sadness returned. The faraway look in his eyes. The pain that he didn't want to discuss, even after all these weeks at home.

The whistle of the teakettle jolted her from her thoughts. Racing to the kitchen, she removed it from the gas and poured the water into the drip pot.

She felt his arms around her waist.

"I'm sorry. Did the teakettle wake you?" she asked.

"Yes, but that's all right. It's our first Christmas together, and I don't want to miss any of it."

Ordinarily, they would have read the newspaper while drinking coffee, but on this important holiday the newspaper was not published, giving all of its employees time at home with their families.

"What would you like for breakfast?" she asked.

"Cornflakes."

"Nothing more special than that?"

"It's the most ordinary things that are special. I used to lie on my bunk and imagine sitting at the breakfast table with you, drinking coffee and, in my daydreams, we were always eating cornflakes."

"Then that's what we'll have."

Later, they exchanged their presents. Mary Grace had knitted her husband a vest of royal blue wool. He gave her a sterling silver chain with a white enamelled flower on it.

"It's called edelweiss, and it's a symbol of Austria," he explained. "I bought it last winter, too late to send it for Christmas, so I decided to put it away and save it for today."

It was time to get dressed for church. Sam wore the royal blue vest over a pale blue collared shirt, and Mary Grace wore a yellow sweater and her edelweiss.

The priest spoke at length about the trials that the country had so recently come through, about the need for tolerance and compassion for the many displaced persons (Mary Grace hated the term "DPs"), and, inevitably, he spoke of the men who had died and were remembered on this day.

Mary felt Sam's body stiffen and saw him bite his

lower lip.

They came home from church, and she put a small roast into the oven. Her family had wanted Mary Grace and Sam to join them for Christmas dinner, but she had explained that she wanted to have him all to herself, just this once.

"I think I'll take a walk in the park," he said.

"I'll come with…"

"No, please. I need to be by myself for awhile."

She watched out the window as he walked down their street, his shoulders sagging, his head down, the wind blowing through his dark hair now streaked with gray although he was only thirty.

She went into their bedroom and opened the drawer that held his letters from all those years that he had been gone. It was a large, deep drawer but nevertheless stuffed with envelopes tied in batches by month. For most of the war, he had written to her every second day, but last summer there had been weeks when she had heard nothing. She had been frantic with worry, and then it had come, the letter now tied with a black ribbon, the letter which explained all of the pain that he had felt, that he still felt.

June 10, 1945
Austria

Hello, Darling

I hope you are well and aren't worried. I guess you must feel pretty bad about not getting any mail for the last few weeks.

Honey, I tried to write, but I just couldn't bring myself to send the letters. Everything seems to have dropped out of things for the last few weeks…I seem lost but now that I've made up my mind to finally send this letter I just might as well write the whole thing.

I hope Ethel is taking it all right. I know what a blow it is to her. I should write to her, but I know it would be harder for me to write to her than to you. You can tell her or let her read this. I have a letter written by Gross, who is in the hospital with bad burns from the accident. I could send the letter when I write to Ethel.

You know how much I thought of Paul. It just about floored me when I realized that Paul was dead. I don't know just how to start the explanation, so I'll start with a few days before.

The evening of May 19 there was a call from Higher Headquarters for us to lay a line to another Group. We were to do it on Monday morning, May 21. It was quite a long line, so we started two trucks from opposite ends. Paul started from the other Group headquarters and started laying back toward Gielow and I. It was a toss up of who I would be with, but as Paul had the most men I went with Gielow and drove his truck. We had laid about two miles of wire and decided to go and look for Paul and his crew to find out which road he was approaching us on as there were quite a few roads that he could be coming down. Kuehn, Gielow, and I got in a Jeep and started out to hunt for Paul. We searched quite a few roads but didn't find him so we went to the Group headquarters that Paul started working from.

When we got there, they told us something was the matter with the telephone line, that it was charged with a heavy load of electricity. It had burnt up two of their switchboards. We just laughed thinking that Paul had laid his telephone wire over a house light line and would get a surprise when he went to make a splice in the wire. It had happened a few times before. We never dreamed what we would find.

While we were tracing out the route Paul had taken we stopped to watch some P47s diving close to the ground, then we took off again on Paul's tracks. We got about half a mile away from Paul's truck, which we could see on another road, when an ambulance pulled up beside it. We knew then something serious was wrong so we just took off across open fields to get there quicker. As we pulled up near them the doctor was leaning over Paul who was lying beside the right front wheel of the truck. Gross was lying about thirty feet away out in the field like he was dead and St. George was staggering around in circles just crying his eyes out. He hollered for us not to touch the wire or the truck because they were both hot. I ran to Gross thinking it was Paul. He was as gray as a sheet and just coming to. I thought he was dead. I then ran to where Paul was lying with the doctor feeling his pulse. At the time I didn't realize what the doctor said but later on I realized what he meant. He said there wasn't any pulse. I still didn't think Paul was dead. I knelt down and tried to talk to him but he was just as still as dead. I still thought he was just knocked cold. I picked up his head and shoulders and helped put him in the ambulance. I still didn't think he was dead. After they had loaded Gross in beside Paul, the ambulance left. We cut the wire with an ax so as to de-charge the truck. St. George then told us how it happened.

He said they had laid the line and had just made an overhead crossing from the telephone pole where the electric wires were. They never thought that the wires were hot. So they stopped to watch the same planes that we were watching earlier. Paul had left to get on the truck and drive it further down the road. None of the other fellows were with him. Well, Paul grabbed the truck to climb on, he was still standing on the ground when he grabbed the truck and so made a perfect ground for the shock. The boys heard him yell like he was choking. Gross ran up to him and asked him what was wrong. You know how you will hit a person on the back when he is choking? Well, Gross grabbed Paul by one arm and hit him on the back and at the same time started to choke himself, he was stuck fast to Paul with the charge going through him. St. George at the same time took a quick swipe at both. He must have realized that they were getting shocked. He said when he hit them everything turned black and he could see the ground throwing sparks and come up to meet him and his shoes started to get hot. The other fellow yelled for help and some fellows down the road called the ambulance and came running to help. In the meantime, the bump St. George had given Paul and Gross caused them to fall. Gross fell first and Paul stood for about a minute longer, then he fell. St. George dragged Gross away as he was moving around and maybe would have bumped into the truck again. Paul was lying perfectly still about a foot away from the truck on his back. That was just the time the ambulance pulled up and we got there just a minute after.

I drove the truck back to the battery and went to the chaplain right away. I wanted to find out how bad Paul was hurt. So we got in a Jeep and drove to the hospital. It was there that I finally realized that Paul was dead.

I just became so stunned I couldn't drive. I am not ashamed to admit it but I cried like a baby. It seemed to relieve me and so I got back to the battery and collected his personal belongings. He had over four hundred dollars in his purse and lots of things we thought Ethel would want. I still have a box of his souvenirs which I'm sending this week. I thought that it was already gone but when I got back from Paris it was still in the supply room.

I did all I could to give Paul a decent funeral. Father Healy held the services. The boys are buried in a sort of sack, and I didn't like that idea. I got permission to make a casket so Paul was buried in a good strong box with a pillow and new blanket that I was going to send home. Paul is buried in a military cemetery at Ulm, Germany. I got permission to have a military funeral at the cemetery so we took the big bus that we have in the battery and about fourteen fellows got permission to attend. It took us eight hours going and eight hours coming back because it is 200 miles one way.

I'll always feel that Paul knows I tried my best to give him his right burial. Maybe I could have done more but I don't know much of Army regulations on that subject.

Paul was the most liked fellow in the battery by officers and enlisted men. Everyone cooperated in every way to help in his last rites. He was the only boy in our group of over 1000 men ever to receive such a grand funeral. We fired thirty rounds over his grave and Father Healy gave him a Catholic Mass.

I hope his mother and Ethel will understand that I did all in my power to do the right thing and I want them to know that Paul was laid away with a real civilian church funeral.

I know Paul never knew what happened. The doctor said he died instantly with no pain.

Gross is burnt pretty bad from the elbow to his shoulder blade. The shoulder blade bone is scorched so he will be in the hospital for a long time. It just melted the rubber soles off his shoes.

Honey, I hope you will help me out in explaining to Ethel. I only regret that I couldn't have been there when it happened. The only consolation I've got is that I could help pick him up and try to give him a decent funeral.

Gross and St. George I think will get the Soldier's medal.

It makes me feel awful that the war was over and everyone safe from harm of war and starting to relax when this terrible accident had to happen.

They sent me to Paris, as I've told you, to relax. I didn't want to go as it wasn't my turn but the captain thought it best that I get away for awhile.

So, Darling, with this letter written I can feel a heavy load lifting from my shoulders. I hope it will ease Ethel's mind and Paul's mother's. I hope and pray that they recover from the shock of his untimely death.

I guess I'll close for now, hoping this letter passes on to you.

Say hello to everyone. So with loads of love, I remain,

Your loving husband,
Sam

Mary Grace cried, just as she had when the letter arrived. She knew now that the months had not taken away Sam's pain, that he was still suffering. And she wondered how many men across the country were suffering from memories of things they had seen, things they had done. She wondered if men would always feel that they had to hold back their tears, that they had to be strong around their women.

She put the letter back into the drawer. Outside wet flakes of snow were falling. She pulled on her boots, grabbed her coat, and headed down the street to the park.

He was sitting on a bench at the duck pond, his chin on his chest, his eyes staring at the ground. Wordlessly, she sat beside him and took his cold, ungloved hand. He looked at her with gray eyes swimming in pools of tears.

"Don't you think it's time we talked about Paul?" she asked.

"I…can't."

"I think you have to. Please don't shut me out. It's more than just his dying, isn't it?"

He took a deep breath and squeezed her hand.

"I keep thinking that it was just the luck of the draw that I wasn't with him, that I went on the other truck. I could have been killed with him."

"And you feel guilty about that?" she asked.

"Yeah. I guess I do. Why was I left alive?"

"Maybe it was so you could give him a really special funeral. Did you ever think of that, Sam? You were the best friend any man could have ever wanted, and I'm proud of you for caring so much."

He began to sniffle and gulp air.

She pulled his head to her chest and whispered, "Go ahead, Sam. Cry it out."

As his body heaved with sobs, she held him. And she felt closer to him than ever before.

The Fallout Shelter

1952

It was Jimmy's idea.

Jimmy's my brother.

"Me and Mary Agnes want to camp out in the fallout shelter," he said. "Can we, Mom, huh?"

Mom started to protest but he said, "When the Russians drop the bomb, we're gonna be in there for days, maybe weeks! It would be better if we were used to it already."

The fallout shelter had been installed in the back yard of our house in La Habra, California, the previous summer.

Mom said we'd have to ask Dad, so we ran down the street to the drugstore. Dad was talking to a man in a dark blue suit. Jimmy started to talk, but Dad put his finger to his lips to tell us to be quiet.

"Dick, these are my children, Jimmy and Mary Agnes. Kids, this is Mr. Nixon. He used to be our senator, but next month he's going to be Vice President of the United States."

Jimmy said, "Wow! The whole United States?"

The stranger nodded and smiled. "With that red hair and all those freckles, you two could be in a Norman Rockwell painting."

I was pleased. The walls of my room were plastered with Saturday Evening Post covers, and sometimes I dreamed about being a famous artist like Mr. Rockwell.

"Me and Mary Agnes want to camp out in the fallout shelter," Jimmy said. "Can we, Dad?"

Dad started to shake his head, so I asked, "Mr. Nixon, you got any kids?"

"Yes, I do. Two little girls."

"You'd let them sleep overnight in your fallout

shelter, wouldn't you?"

"How old are you, Mary Agnes?"

"I'm nine, Sir. Jimmy's eleven."

He leaned over and spoke in a loud voice, loud enough for Dad to hear. "My girls are six and four, so they're too little. But if they were nine and eleven, why, sure, I'd let them do it!" And he winked at me.

Dad said we'd talk about it later at home. "You two run along now," he said.

"Bye, Mr. Nixon. Hope you like being President!" I said.

"Vice President," Jimmy corrected me.

I don't think Mom liked the idea of our sleeping in the shelter, but Dad said we could. While I set the table for dinner, I thought about what I wanted to take with me. My Raggedy Ann doll and my furry slippers with the bunny faces on them and my pillow.

After dinner, Dad gave us a good talking to. He called it "ground rules".

First off, Dad told Jimmy that if I wanted to come out of the shelter, he had to let me.

"And no scary stories either, Jim," he said sternly.

Mom said we weren't allowed to open any cans. "I don't want you cutting yourselves, and we need the cans in case…in case…well, we need the cans. Besides, I'm going to make you some sandwiches."

"Peanut butter and jelly?" I asked.

"Peanut butter and jelly, for sure," Mom said.

After dinner we got our things together and went outside to the shelter. Dad lifted the "hatch", that's what he called the door in the ground, and went in first to turn on the one light bulb that hung by a cord from the ceiling. It was powered by a generator. He held my slippers and pillow and Raggedy Ann while I climbed down the ladder.

The shelter was just one room made out of cinder blocks. There were two sets of bunk beds, and underneath each one were cases of canned food like soup and chili con carne and fruit cocktail. There was a little stove that ran on Sterno and jugs of water everywhere. Our old kitchen table and four chairs, the ones we used before Dad bought Mom a new set, were in the middle of the room. Shelves held games and books and comic books and several flashlights.

When Dad was ready to leave, he said to Jimmy, "I'm going to close the hatch from the outside. You make sure you can push it open from inside when you want to come out."

I could tell it was heavy, but Jimmy managed.

"Good night," Dad called as he closed us in.

I looked around. It seemed different. Of course, I had only been in there during the day with the hatch open and light shining in. It looked a lot smaller now. I sat down, clutching my doll closer.

"You okay?" Jimmy asked me.

"I guess so."

"You look like you might throw up."

"I'll be okay. It's just that it's smaller in here than I remembered."

"You must have that phobia thing."

"What?" I asked.

"Phobia means being scared of something. Like spiders. In your case it's called...well, I forget but it sounds like Santa Claus."

I had no idea why anyone would be scared of Santa

Claus or what it had to do with the fallout shelter.

"Come on, Mary Agnes, let's play checkers. It'll take your mind off things."

I beat him three games in a row, and I could tell he wasn't happy about it.

"Let's quit," he said, "I'm getting bored."

"Wish we had a television in here," I muttered. We were the first people on our street to get a television. We thought it was so big. The screen was nine inches across.

"There's probably a radio around here somewhere," he said. "How else would people know when to come out?"

I shivered, wondering who was going to make the announcement if the bomb had killed everybody above ground.

"What time do you think it is?" I asked.

"You big baby! I knew you wouldn't stick it out."

"I just asked what time it was."

He found a clock, but it had stopped at 2:05. It needed to be wound up, but since we didn't know what time it was that was pointless.

At least that's what he said.

"It is <u>not</u> pointless," I said. "We can guess what time it is now and set the clock to that. When did we get in here?"

"About seven o'clock."

"Okay, we've been in here maybe four hours, so let's say it's eleven o'clock."

"You're so dumb, Mary Agnes. We haven't been here four hours. We'd be lots sleepier if it was eleven o'clock. I'd say nine o'clock."

"Let's say ten o'clock," I suggested, but then he

said nine-thirty. I could have gone on arguing, but it wasn't that big a deal. We made it nine-thirty.

"Wish we had a television in here," I said again.

"Hey, 'member that thing about the bomb on Ed Sullivan a couple weeks ago?" Jimmy asked.

I remembered. And I didn't want to. "Stop it, Jimmy!"

He laughed and said "Do you 'member that cloud, the mushroom cloud, and then the faces of all the people watching it and they turned to skeletons and..."

"STOP IT!!!" I said, putting my hands over my ears. "Dad told you no scary stories."

"He meant made up ones like ghost stories. Not television."

My hands on my ears couldn't block out his voice.

"And that bug, that moth, flying around the flame and then the flame went out and..."

With my hands still over my ears I began to sing "Jingle Bells" as loud as I could to drown him out. He came over to me and stuck his face right next to mine, and he was laughing.

"You stop right now, Jimmy, or I'm outta here! And I'm gonna tell Dad what you did!"

"Okay, okay. So what do you want to do now?"

We found some comic books to read. And we ate some of the sandwiches.

"Sure is small in here," I said.

"I heard of a lady in Washington, D.C. who has a shelter big enough for fifteen people to stay for two weeks."

"How many kids does she have?" I asked.

"Silly, she doesn't have that many kids. She gives lots of parties and figures whenever the bomb hits anybody visiting them would have to go into the shelter with them. I guess you gotta be careful who you have around 'cause you might be stuck with them for a long time."

Joe Willey came to my mind as someone I wouldn't want to be in a shelter with. When it rained and the worms came out on the walk to school, Joe always threatened to put one down my back. Mom said it meant he liked me, but that was just about the dumbest thing I'd ever heard.

I had to go to the bathroom real bad, but there was just the one room in the shelter and the commode was over in the corner. I sure didn't want to sit on the toilet in front of Jimmy, so I just squeezed my legs together. I guess he must have been going through the same thing because he said, "It would be pretty bad if you had to go to the bathroom."

I agreed it would but said that the problem was bound to come up if people were in the shelter for days.

"I gotta go," he said. "You turn around and face the wall, Mary Agnes. Don't peek! And I promise to do the same for you when you have to go."

The matter solved, we decided to try to get some sleep. I put on my bunny slippers and clutched Raggedy Ann as I snuggled under the blankets on the cot. I was sure glad I brought my own pillow. As I started to doze off, I wondered what Mom and Dad were doing right that very minute.

I had bad dreams about mushroom clouds and fire and bugs and checkers falling all over the floor.

I awoke to sunlight streaming through the open hatch and Mom saying, "Well, I didn't think you two would stick it out. How about some breakfast?"

I took off the furry slippers and put my shoes on, grabbed my doll and my pillow, and climbed eagerly into the December sunshine. Jimmy was right behind me.

"So how was it?" she asked.

"Not bad," I said, "but could you hang a curtain or something in front of the commode?"

"That's a good idea," she said as she hugged me.

Syrup on the table meant pancakes, my favorite breakfast in the whole world.

Mom turned the gas on under the griddle. "How many pancakes can you eat, Mary Agnes?"

"A whole bunch, but I'll start with four."

Christmas Birthday

1959

Marie Noel Barker was going to be ten years old on Christmas Day.

One day during the last week of school, she and her friends, Betsy and Trudy and Flo, were jumping rope at recess.

"I don't think I'd like having my birthday on Christmas," Trudy said.

Marie just smiled.

"Have you ever had a birthday party?" Betsy asked.

"Of course! Every year," Marie said as she twirled the rope.

Betsy spoke breathlessly as she jumped. "I've never been invited, have you, Flo? Trudy?" They all shook their heads.

"Well, of course, it's a family party," Marie explained.

"Why doesn't your mother give you a half-birthday party on June 25th?" Flo wanted to know.

"She did once. For my seventh birthday. My seven - and - half, I mean. It was before we moved here. But it just didn't seem like a birthday party, you know?"

"So tell us how you celebrate," Betsy urged.

"Well, on Christmas Eve we go to church. Mom bakes every day for the week before Christmas, all kinds of yummy things. She puts a ham in the oven Christmas Eve afternoon, and when we get home from church we eat it, along with fruit salad, nut breads, pies. On Christmas morning we open our presents."

Marie looked at her friends and asked, "You know how you feel when the last present under the tree has been opened? You feel kinda sad, right? Well, not me! Because there's still lots of presents, and they're all mine!

"For dinner that night, I can decide what we'll have. I usually pick breaded pork chops and yams. And everybody comes, my cousins and aunts and uncles, and not because it's Christmas but for my birthday party."

Trudy asked what the rest were wondering. "But don't some people bring you just one present and tell you it's for Christmas and your birthday?"

"I think it happened a long time ago but not since."

"Probably your mom told 'em not to do that again," Betsy said.

"Yeah, probably your mom," echoed Flo.

"And you know what's the best thing about a Christmas birthday?" Marie asked.

The three friends leaned forward.

"I share it with Jesus."

The bell signalled the end of recess.

That afternoon after school, Marie got her new glasses.

Being one of the smallest in the class, she always sat in the front row where she could see the blackboard. The Monday after Thanksgiving, Mrs. Jenkins, the school nurse, had come into the classroom to check everyone's eyes. One by one, the students went to the back of the room and were asked to read the chart Mrs. Jenkins had put on the front wall.

But Marie had a hard time reading the chart. In fact, even the big **E** was blurry. A trip to the optometrist confirmed that she needed glasses.

She wanted red frames because red was her favorite color.

"But what about the times that you wear a pink dress or your orange sweater?" her mother had asked. "I think you should get these nice brown frames; they'll go with everything."

So she got the brown frames. By recess the next day, one of the boys had called her the dreaded name. Four-Eyes.

She came home and cried. Her mother tried to explain that even when she had been a little girl, the boys had called girls with glasses "Four-Eyes". That didn't help at all.

During lunch the next day, Trudy asked where the glasses were.

"In my pocket," Marie said. "I really only need them for reading."

"But you wore them all day yesterday," Flo said.

"That was just because I forgot the case at home."

The following day was Saturday. Mom, Dad, Marie, and her little sister Debbie went shopping. First to the five-and-ten and then to Bressmer's Department Store to see Santa Claus.

"Where are your glasses?" her mother asked.

"At home."

"But what are they doing at home?"

"I only need them for reading anyway."

Her mother opened her mouth to argue but instead just rolled her eyes.

In the five-and-ten they bought new mittens for Debbie, slippers for Dad for Christmas, and jelly beans. Marie was so busy looking at the candy in the glass case that she didn't hear her mother say that it was time to go.

Marie looked all through the case at the licorice,

nonpareils, taffy, and rainbow mints before she realized that her mother and sister weren't there. She wandered through the store looking for them, first one aisle, then another. Panic set in, and she was close to tears.

She bumped into a child and apologized, "Oh, excuse me, Little Boy." Squinting, she said, "Or are you a little girl? Oh my gosh, you're a mannequin!"

She heard giggles behind her. Debbie. Her mother.

"Now will you believe me when I say you need glasses for more than just reading? We'll have to go home and get them before we go to Bressmer's."

By the time they reached the top floor of the store where Santa was, the line was long.

A girl with her little brother stood in line behind Marie and Debbie. She had glasses, too.

"I wanted red ones like yours," Marie said, "but my mom said brown was more practical."

"I wouldn't have got these either except for Grandma. She told Dad to let me have the color I wanted since I have to wear them all the time."

Two boys passed by. One called out, "Hey, Janet! Janet Four-Eyes!"

The girl with the red glasses shouted back, "Shut up, Jeffrey!"

"What are you gonna ask Santa for?" Debbie asked Marie.

"I think a pair of glasses like Janet's, an extra pair." Turning to her new friend, she said, "And if not for Christmas, then for my birthday. It's the same day."

"Really?" Janet squealed. "Mine, too! I'm going to

be eleven." She wrinkled her nose. "Isn't a Christmas birthday the pits?"

Marie smiled.

"Oh, no. It's wonderful! Let me tell you how my family and I celebrate…"

Christmas Walk

1960

Traditionally, after all the presents had been opened, after Christmas dinner had been eaten and cleared away, the Coggin family would stroll through the neighborhood looking at the decorations.

Years ago it had been Mother and Daddy, Jerry, and Marian, but Daddy, preferring to read the latest issue of Sports Illustrated, had dropped out of the walk several years ago. And now that Jerry was married, he and Linda left soon after dinner to get the children home to bed.

Marian and Mother pulled on their boots and coats and gloves and started up the street.

Most of the houses were decorated exactly the same, the standard for that time, with large red, blue, and green lights outlining the roofs and occasionally a tree in the front yard.

They passed the Corcorans, and Marian asked how they were.

"The boys are married now, of course," Mother replied, "and Jane Corcoran works in the school cafeteria with me. Joe had a stroke and had to retire early, and she couldn't bear having him underfoot all day long, so she works 10 'til 2, and it gets her out of the house and adds some money to his pension."

Marian was still surprised that her stay-at-home mother now had a job as supervisor of the cafeteria in the new junior high school, which opened the year she entered Penn State.

"How does Daddy feel about your working?" she asked.

"Actually he's been terrific about it. He used to say that he'd never let any wife of his get a job, but I think he's proud of me. I guess you're going to work for awhile after you and Ted get married."

Marian took off her glove and looked at the diamond engagement ring which sparkled in the glow of the street light. She'd had it since her birthday, September 1st.

"Yes, I'll work until we start a family and then again after the kids are grown. Maybe I'll be able to work part time in between."

"If you had gotten a degree in nursing or teaching like I suggested, you'd probably be able to, but how many part-time jobs for economists do you think there are?"

Marian bit her lip. She and her mother disagreed on a number of things, and she knew it would just get worse as they began to plan the wedding. Already her mother was working on a huge guest list, insisting that she had to ask her cousins to be bridesmaids, frowning when Marian mentioned a garden wedding at home with daisies in the bridesmaids' hair.

"You know, Dear," her mother said, "I think your father was disappointed that Ted didn't ask his permission to marry you before giving you that ring."

"Mother, now you know that's not true. Daddy said he thought it was wonderful the way Ted asked me. You're the one who thinks it should have been done differently. Don't go blaming it on Daddy. People don't do that anymore, Mother, just like they don't register for sterling silver flatware. At least my friends don't. We're all much too practical. Besides, pewter is lovely and doesn't need to be polished. If anyone asks about silverware, tell them I'd rather have pewter."

They walked farther down the street. More red, blue, and green lights, occasionally some orange. No one seemed to try to outshine their neighbors, which was nice.

Mother changed the subject. "So did you vote in the election?"

"Well, of course I did! It was the first time I could, and I wouldn't have missed it. I think there are great times ahead for America."

"So you voted for Kennedy?"

"Sure. Who were you for, Mother?"

"Who was I for or who did I vote for?"

"Well, they're the same thing, aren't they?"

Mother chuckled. "Not in our house. I guess Daddy and I never told you; we were afraid it would leak out. You see, Daddy's a Democrat, and I'm a Republican. But when he became a boss in the mine about twelve years ago, they told him that since he was now part of management, he had to vote Republican. He was always afraid that somehow they would find out if he didn't vote like they said and then he'd lose his job. So, when he goes into the voting booth, he votes straight Republican for me and I vote straight Democratic for him."

Marian stopped under a street light and stared at her mother. "But you just cancel out each other's votes!"

"Well, we would anyway, if we voted the way we each wanted to. So it doesn't matter."

"So you don't like John Kennedy?"

"It's not that I don't like him, but he's so young to be President. Actually I prefer Richard Nixon. I like his wife. She's so down-to-earth, you know? And I don't think anyone with small children should be in the White House, not a good environment for the kids.

Like living in a goldfish bowl."

"Mother, did it ever occur to you that you could tell Daddy you voted for him but not do it, just vote the way you want? That way, the candidate you like would have a better chance."

It was Mother's turn to be surprised. "Marian! Your father entrusts me with his vote. There are other things just about as sacred as our wedding vows. You'll find out after you marry Ted. I do like him, you know. And I do want you to have your kind of wedding. As we've been walking, I've been remembering how my mother tried to take over mine. And how I resented it."

Marian breathed a sigh of relief and pulled her mother closer.

They had reached the end of the street.

"Would you look at that!" Mother exclaimed.

The DeSimone house did not have the traditional red, blue, and green lights outlining the roof. Instead they were white, all white. And the same lights were in the tree near the driveway.

"They say she has her dining room walls painted orange."

"Oh, Mother, you've got to be kidding!"

"No, I'm not. And they don't have a real tree inside. It's silver metallic. Of course it can't have any electric lights. and all of the balls are purple. I'm not making this up. Helen is the Avon lady, and she saw it all with her own eyes. She said Caroline DeSimone told her that it's the wave of the future."

Marian began to laugh. "White lights? Artificial Christmas trees? That'll be the day!"

We Wish You a Merry Tonsillectomy

1963

"...so that's why Mary Jane's having trouble hearing? She needs her tonsils and adenoids to come out?" Mummy put a protective arm around her seven-year old.

The doctor nodded as he dialed the telephone. He was tall and bald, had a huge stomach, and smelled of pipe tobacco. Mary Jane didn't like him one bit. He was even worse than the dentist who wanted to pull out her tooth. But she had carried on so much that Daddy had said to Mummy that they should just forget it for now. Mary Jane was convinced that it would be the same with the tonsils and "annoys".

"This is Dr. Shelby. I want to reserve a bed and operating room on December 27th for a tonsillectomy and adenoidectomy for one Mary Jane Pulaski, date of birth 04-04-56."

Mary Jane glared at him and said in a loud voice, "How many Mary Jane Pulaskis does he think there are?"

"Shhh," Mummy whispered.

On December 27th Mummy and Daddy took Mary Jane to the hospital. They packed her slippers and her hairbrush and her favorite teddy bear in the little pink suitcase that she had taken to Grandma's the one time she had tried to stay overnight. The family still talked about that day. She had been so excited to be a "big girl" until it started to get dark. By the time Uncle Jack took her home at eight o'clock, she had written six letters to her parents and promised that she'd never be away from them again.

She didn't like the hospital. It was all gray and white and cold. They took her to a room called a "ward" that had seven beds in it and made her put on a nightshirt that was open in the back.

"I know it's scary, Honey," Daddy said, "but you're going to be the second one to have your tonsils out. It's better to do it soon than to be one of the last. By the time the seventh child comes back, you'll have it all over with and be in great shape. And I'll be here when you wake up, I promise."

But Mary Jane was not Number 2. Somehow things got mixed up, and she was the very last one. She watched each of the other children come back and be sick when they woke up and heard them complain about how much their throats hurt.

Finally some people came for her and transferred her to a table on wheels. She was rolled through the hallways of the hospital, and once she tried to jump off and run away.

In the operating room she saw Dr. Shelby putting a white mask over his face. Like the bad man in the cowboy shows on television.

Somebody put a cone over her nose, and she smelled something sweet, but not nice sweet. Yucky sweet.

And then she was falling down a well, falling, falling. At the bottom was the crocodile from Peter Pan, and he was opening his mouth to catch her. His mouth opened wider and wider, and she was falling faster and faster…Oh!

Just as she was about to be swallowed up, she opened her eyes, and there was Daddy with some red flowers in his hand.

Her throat hurt. She moved her tongue around in her mouth, and her eyes got bigger.

"I ah ah ho in mah mah."

"What's that?" Daddy asked.

"I got a hole in my mouth!"

Mummy laughed. "We asked Dr. Shelby to pull out the tooth."

"But nobody asked me!"

"We figured you wouldn't mind." Daddy said, patting her hand.

One of the other fathers came over and said he was going out for ice cream for all of the children and asked what kind Mary Jane would like.

"That's very kind," Mummy said. "She loves strawberry."

The other children were laughing and talking as though this were a great adventure.

"How's your ice cream, Honey?" Daddy asked.

"It's okay, but I want some real food."

"You won't be able to have anything solid for about three days."

A nurse came over and said that the parents would have to leave now, that it was time to get the little patients ready for bed.

"What do you mean?" Mummy asked. "I plan to stay here with her."

"I'm sorry, but you can't. Hospital rules."

"But my little girl has never been away from us at night. Not even at her grandmother's. I promised her I'd stay with her."

"Well, Ma'm, I'm sorry. You shouldn't have promised her that. Hospital rules."

Thirty minutes later Mary Jane was bundled up on

the front seat of the car between her parents.

"I've never been so embarrassed in my life!" Mummy said. "Imagine being asked to take your child home because she was disrupting the ward and making all the other children cry."

"I guess we should have done a better job of preparing her for this," Daddy said.

"And when she started screaming that the doctor had stolen her tooth and was going to come back to kill her, well, I thought I'd die of shame!"

"Forget it, Carol," Daddy whispered. "It's over now."

As soon as they got home, Mary Jane said she was hungry and wanted some spaghetti.

"No solid food for three days. Just soup and tea," Mummy said.

"I want spaghetti!"

"Look, go on to sleep, and when you wake up, if you still want spaghetti, I'll make you some."

At 3 a.m. Mary Jane got out of her bed and went into her parents' room.

"I'm ready for my spaghetti now."

Daddy whispered as Mummy opened the can, "She can't eat that!"

"Shhh. As soon as she takes one bite, it'll hurt her throat, and she'll go back to bed."

But Mary Jane ate the whole bowl and then the rest of the can.

All I Ever Wanted

1967

There was a chill in the air as I approached the bus stop, but the sun was trying to break through the clouds.

Two other people waited for the bus, and as I drew near I recognized Mrs. Braun and eight-year old Peter.

"Mary Kay!" she exclaimed and kissed my cheek. "When did you get home?"

"Last night."

"And you're going into town so soon?"

"Well," I said, "I haven't done my Christmas shopping yet. How about you? I'd have thought you'd be finished by now."

"I was, but Karen is bringing her fiance home for Christmas, and we need something for him under the tree."

"Karen's engaged? That's wonderful! When are they getting married?'

"Not 'til she finishes college, in a year and a half."

"How's the rest of the family?" I asked.

"Matt's working too hard, same as always. Andrew's a senior now. He just found out he's got a football scholarship to State for next year."

"Oh, I'm so happy for him."

There was an uncomfortable silence for a minute or two. I waited in case she would offer information, but she just stared at her shoes. Finally I went for it.

"And Bob?"

"He's stationed in Saigon."

The bus came.

Peter had a comic book to read, so Mrs. Braun and I sat together. She hadn't changed much in the past couple of years, a little grayer, a little plumper.

"How long has he been in Saigon?" I asked.

"Three months." Her voice trembled.

"It'll be okay," I said. "He'll be okay. I hear Saigon's pretty safe. At least he's not out in the jungle somewhere."

"I know. It's just…"

"I know," I said, squeezing her hand.

She changed the subject. "So how do you like living in Washington?"

"Oh, it's great. Except for the hours. I start at 7:15, so I have to be out the door by six. It takes me two buses to get there."

"Do you have time to see the sights?" she asked.

"Oh, yeah. I go to the Smithsonian almost every week-end."

"Have you ever been on one of those embassy tours? I'd love to do that."

I shook my head. "No, I'm not allowed…" Then I stopped myself.

She whispered, "Because you work for an intelligence agency?"

I nodded.

The bus wound through the village and onto the road along the lake. I thought that missing an embassy tour was the least of my sacrifices. What really rankled me was having to sit back and watch the anti-war demonstrations and not be able to take part in them. But we were cautioned on a regular basis that we were not to be seen anywhere near the demonstrations, not if we wanted to keep our jobs.

I thought, I hate this war! What are we doing there?

The nightly news regularly gave the body counts,

the other side's always much bigger than ours, of course. Thousands, tens of thousands. Numbers. But now not just numbers. Faces. My brother's best friend Mark had been killed in June. I didn't know if my brother would ever get over it. He vacillated between wanting to go and kill 'em all and wanting to escape to Canada. If the war went on much longer, he might not have the choice.

Mrs. Braun interrupted my thoughts. "Are you happy, Mary Kay?"

"Sure, I love Washington."

"What I mean is…oh, never mind. I forgot what I was going to ask."

But she hadn't forgotten. She just didn't know how to ask if I were still in love with her son.

Closing my eyes, I listened to the sound of the bus engine and let myself drift back to high school. I fell in love with Bob Braun in tenth grade when we were in biology together. Old Mr. Hickey had this dumb routine of calling on people to answer questions, and if you didn't know the answer he'd make you stand there until you got one right. It was awful.

On one particular day I had already missed two questions in a row, and if God had given me the option of dying on the spot, I'd have taken it. My hands were sweating, I felt dizzy, and my knees were about to give out.

"Who is called the father of genetics?" Old Mr. Hickey asked me.

We always referred to him as "Old Mr. Hickey." He probably wasn't much past forty, but he had nondescript color eyes and hair and stooped when he walked.

At that moment I was so rattled that I couldn't even remember what genetics were, let alone who their father was. There was a barely perceptible rustle of paper beside me. I glanced down and saw the word MENDEL in big letters.

"Mendel," I blurted out.

"Correct. You may sit down," my tormentor said.

I sank into my seat, then glanced at the face above the paper. Bob Braun. He smiled. I rolled my eyes and mouthed the word "thanks".

He started out helping me with biology, and by summer we were going steady. I was at his house much of the time and loved his family as much as I loved him. Mr. Braun, Matthew Braun, was the grade school principal. He was the most soft-spoken man I've ever known, and yet no one questioned his authority. The Brauns had four children—Bob, Karen, Andrew, and Peter.

During my junior and senior years my goal was to be Bob Braun's wife. It's all I ever wanted…that, and to stay in Centerville. Other people couldn't wait to leave, but I loved it. It was a place where you felt safe, far away from big-city crime. Once, when we went to visit Aunt Josie in Chicago, a man stole Mom's purse. But in Centerville we left our doors unlocked, day and night. Everyone knew everyone else, all two thousand of us. Of course, there wasn't much for young people to do. Ice skate and sled in winter, swim at Foley's Pond or in the lake in summer. All the boys looked forward to the day when they could drive because half an hour away there were movie theaters and fast-food restaurants and a miniature golf course.

After he got his license, Bob fixed up an old car,

and we had many wonderful evenings in it. But that car was the beginning of the end for us. We now had a way to get to Inspiration Point, on the north side of the lake, where all the kids went to park. Bob began to say things like "If you loved me, you'd prove it". Love him or not, that was something I wouldn't do. Not 'til after marriage, I hinted. I would have married him in a minute, but he kept saying he wasn't ready. And then came the night he brought me home early after taunting, "If you won't, I'll find someone who will!"

"Go ahead, see if I care!" I had yelled as his car screeched over the gravel of my driveway.

Graduation was two nights later. As I adjusted my cap, Bob came up behind me. "Can I talk to you for a minute?" he asked.

My heart raced. Oh, it's going to be okay, I thought as I followed him to the alcove near the janitor's closet.

"I'm sorry about the other night," he began.

"It's okay," I said as I wrapped my arms around his waist.

He pushed me away. "No, it's not. I respect your decision, but I just can't be that close to you anymore. It's not going to work out."

"What are you saying?" I felt like I had been punched in the stomach.

"I'm going away, Mary Kay. To Cleveland, to work for my Uncle Jack."

The beginning notes of the processional interrupted our conversation. I looked for him after the ceremony, but he was gone. The next Sunday in church Father Dennis asked us all to remember Bob Braun in our prayers as he began a new job and a new life.

I started secretarial school in July as planned. There were countless rides on the bus, time for me to ponder what had happened.

I used to stop in at the Brauns "just to say hello", hoping to get news of him. Once when we were all on the porch drinking lemonade, I offered to go to the kitchen for more ice. When no one was looking, I raced to Bob's bedroom to see if my picture were still on his dresser. I was elated not to see it; he must have taken it with him.

I don't remember how I found out that he got married.

The thing I had always liked best about Centerville was that everyone knew everyone else. Now the thing I hated most about Centerville was that everyone knew me, knew that my boyfriend, the one I wanted to marry, had gotten another girl pregnant and had to marry her. And they all knew my heart was broken.

I just had to get out of Centerville. Grandma suggested that I go to Washington after finishing my secretarial course. She gave me enough money to stay at the YWCA while I looked for a job and an apartment.

I have to admit my hopes rose when I heard that Sally, his wife, lost the baby. If there ever was a baby. She wouldn't have been the first girl to trap a guy into marrying her that way. I used to fantasize that Bob would show up on my doorstep and beg me to forgive him and to marry him. In my dreams he always told me that marrying Sally had been a mistake, that she wasn't pregnant after all, that he was going to divorce her. I never thought about having to leave the church if I married a divorced man. What would I have chosen if it came down to that, Bob or the church? The choice was never mine to make. The last I heard, he had enlisted.

The traffic lights ahead meant that we were reaching our destination. As we prepared to get off the bus, I said to Mrs. Braun, "Tell the family I said hello."

"Why don't you come tell them yourself? How long will you be home?"

"I'm going back Sunday."

"So stop over after Christmas."

"All right, I will. But I'll see you all before that, at Midnight Mass."

"Of course. Bye, Mary Kay."

"Bye, Mrs. Braun. Have a good day."

It was snowing as my family and I drove to church on Christmas Eve. It was my favorite service of the whole year. You had to go early to get a seat, unless you were willing to sit on a folding chair in the aisle. Mr. Braun played the organ for the church, and on Christmas Eve he'd start maybe forty minutes early. It was such a peaceful, glorious time. The wonderful old songs, the smell of evergreens, the flickering candles, everyone huddling together for warmth. On two Christmas Eves I had been with Bob and the rest of his family in the front pew.

But this night the organ was silent as we walked into the church, and the front pew was empty. There were murmurs among the parishioners as everyone wondered what was going on. We sat in silence, and then just before midnight Father Dennis came out and stood in front of the communion rail. His eyes were red, and his hands shook.

"My dear friends," he said with difficulty, "I have sad news, very sad news. This evening the Brauns received word that their son Bob was killed in Vietnam. He was in the barracks when it was bombed."

I had never fainted before, but now my brother Bud was pushing my head down between my knees. As I came to, I heard him whisper to Dad that he would take me home and then come back, but Dad said that he and Mom would get a ride home from Father Dennis.

Outside I leaned against the building and gulped the cold air. I lifted my face to the black sky and let the snowflakes fall on my closed eyelids and melt in my tears.

In a few minutes Bud and I were in the car, heading for home.

"Did I make a complete fool of myself in there?" I asked him.

"No. Everyone was so struck by the news that they didn't even notice you."

If it were a lie, I blessed him for it.

"You've never gotten over him, have you, Mary Kay?"

"I guess not. Funny, I always thought he'd come back to me."

We stayed in the car in the driveway for a long time while I cried on Bud's shoulder.

We went into the kitchen and sat at the table filled with the food that would end our Christmas Eve fast. Nut breads, Mom's ambrosia fruit salad, cold ham. I mindlessly reached for a slice of meat and began to eat.

"I wonder if he was awake when it happened."

"Probably not," Bud said. "It must have happened in the middle of the night. Army barracks are pretty dreary, not the kind of place to hang around. At least, that's what Mark told me." He winced.

"Do you still think about going to Canada?" I asked.

"Yeah. All the time."

"So why don't you?"

He drew a deep breath. "If I go, it'll be forever. I'll never be able to come back here. Mom and Dad fight about that a lot. She wants me to go because I'll be safe. Dad says it would disgrace the family. Damn it, Mary Kay, he thinks this is World War II all over again! I hate it when he says 'right or wrong my country'. This isn't a war against a madman like Hitler. We're not fighting to save our way of life. It's just a dirty little war in a far-off place where the enemy looks just like the good guys. We don't belong there! I hate being put in a position where I either have to go and kill people who haven't done anything to me or else give up everything I love for the rest of my life."

He looked me straight in the eye and said, "No matter what I decide, I'm giving up my life as it is now. Nothing will ever be the same."

He poured eggnog from a carton into two glasses.

"I think you should go, Bud. Canada's not that far away, and we can visit you there. And who knows? Maybe someday, when it's all over, you'll be able to come back."

My parents and I went to see the Brauns on the 26th. Karen and her fiance Mike were in the process of dismantling the Christmas tree. I helped while my parents and Mr. and Mrs. Braun went into the kitchen.

After a few minutes Karen whispered something to Mike, and he left the room.

"So how's life in Washington, Mary Kay?" she asked, her voice cracking. Her eyes behind her glasses were red and swollen.

I told her briefly about my job and my apartment.

"Are you involved with anyone?"

I shook my head.

Her voice was just a whisper. "You were still in love with him, weren't you? My brother."

I nodded.

"I thought so. Had you heard from him recently?"

"Karen, I've never heard from him. Never. Not since graduation, and that was almost three years ago."

"Then I think I'd better tell you. Sally, his wife, lost the baby."

"I heard."

"On his last trip home, he came alone, he said he was going to divorce her. They had a terrible argument, him and Mom and Dad. Dad said he couldn't cast Sally aside because it didn't turn out the way he wanted. Marriage is forever, that's what Dad and Mom kept telling him. No one mentioned you, but I think we all figured that once he was divorced he wanted to find you."

I dug my fingernails into my palm to keep from crying.

"And, then," she continued, "a couple of weeks later he called to say he'd enlisted."

We sat in silence for several minutes before my curiosity compelled me to ask, "What's she like?"

"Sally? She's real nice, Mary Kay. You'd like her."

What an absurd statement, I thought.

"I feel sorry for her," Karen said. "I think she really loved him. I've talked to her occasionally on the phone since he shipped out, and I gather he had written to her only a couple of times. She seemed to know their marriage was over. She's the one they notified, you know. His next of kin. She called us on Christmas Eve. I answered the phone. I thought she was calling to wish us a Merry Christmas..." Karen began to sob and took her glasses off. I touched her shoulder, not knowing how to comfort her.

My parents were calling me to come home.

I hugged her. "Thanks, Karen. Thanks for telling me. It helps to know he cared for me. I always felt he did, but it helps to know. You're right. I never stopped loving him."

We drove home in silence. My heart ached with sorrow for Bob's death and for what might have been. But in there with the pain was this little shred of happiness, knowing he loved me. I wondered if he had thought about me that night before he fell asleep, fell asleep for the last time.

The house was dark when we got back. Bud must be out with his friends, I thought.

Dad picked up the newspaper from the driveway and carried it to the kitchen. Mom set up the ironing board. I headed upstairs to my room.

The open door to Bud's empty closet caught my eye. There was a white envelope on his plaid bedspread, propped up against the pillow. It was addressed to "Mom, Dad, and Mary Kay". My fingers trembled as I pulled out the single sheet of paper.

I felt tremendous sadness for the decision he had made and for the physical distance that would be between us. But also relief. He wouldn't, he couldn't end up like Bob and Mark. There would be some, Dad among them, who would call him a coward, but I thought it had taken great courage to refuse to do what he thought was wrong.

I headed for the kitchen.

"He's gone," I said.

A Humbling Experience

1971

Mitzi Chandler had been flattered when asked to be the director of the Sunday School. The pastor told her that she had the organizational skills and energy to be a great success. And since she was working only two or three days a week as a substitute teacher, she had the time.

She started on Labor Day weekend and was pleased that all of the Sunday School teachers were willing to stay on. This was going to be easy, after all.

On Wednesday evening of the second week, Mitzi got a phone call from Vanessa Bartlett.

"I have to give up my class. Sorry. The doctor's office where I've been working on Tuesdays wants me full-time starting next week. I just won't be able to teach Sunday School anymore."

"But, Vanessa, you're not working on Sunday mornings, are you?"

"No, but I just don't have the time, Mitzi. I'm sorry."

"Well, you'll stay until I find someone, won't you?"

"Sorry. We're going to see Dick's parents this week-end."

Mitzi had a difficult time being nice to Vanessa after that. Oh, she was never unkind, but she wasn't warm and friendly. In truth, she blamed Vanessa for starting what turned out to be a terrible Fall. During the month of October, Mitzi only went to church once. For both services every Sunday she served as a last-minute stand-in for some teacher or other who didn't show up or who called on Sunday morning with some excuse which Mitzi considered flimsy. She began to see herself as a martyr and made sure that everyone knew how hard she was working at this volunteer job.

Things didn't get much better as the holidays neared. Everyone was busier than usual, and it was harder to get substitutes for Sunday mornings.

And it was Vanessa's fault. She started it all.

On Christmas Eve, Mitzi arrived early to be sure that the nursery was open and staffed. There were a few minutes before people would begin arriving, so she went into the church and sat in the back pew. The lights on the Christmas tree sparkled, and the smell of pine boughs filled the sanctuary.

She was aware of someone standing beside her. Vanessa and her husband.

"Merry Christmas," Mitzi said coolly.

"Merry Christmas. We'd like you to do us a favor," Vanessa said.

Mitzi was prepared to refuse, no matter what the request was. She'd show Vanessa that she could say no, too.

"Dick got a surprise bonus for Christmas. We're so blessed, and we wanted to share. We went to the toy store this afternoon and bought things for the Jeffers and McDowell children. I know the church gave them food baskets, but we were afraid they wouldn't have many toys for the kids. We just got back from hiding the presents in the bushes near the front door at each house, but we need for you to tell them that Santa Claus left them there. Please don't let on who did it."

Mitzi, nodding as Vanessa hugged her, felt like crawling under a rock. She was overwhelmed by the amount of money that Vanessa and Dick had spent on toys for six children but even more so when she thought of being in a toy store on Christmas Eve. The crowds must have been horrendous. And the couple wanted to remain anonymous about their generosity.

Mitzi found Mrs. Jeffers in the nursery where she was leaving the baby.

"Santa Claus wants me to tell you that he left some toys for the children in the bushes near your front door," she whispered.

"Oh, Mitzi, how kind you are!"

"I had nothing to do with it, unfortunately."

She waited in the back of the church for the McDowells. Her own family arrived, and she asked them to save her a place.

When the McDowells came, she pulled the father aside and told him about the toys.

"How can we ever thank you?" he asked.

"It wasn't me. Honest. It's another couple in the church who did it. They had a bonus and wanted to share their good fortune with someone having a hard time this Christmas."

"Will you tell them how very grateful we are?" Mr. McDowell asked?

"I certainly will. Merry Christmas."

The choir sang more beautifully than ever, but Mitzi didn't hear them. She was lost in thought. She had been very unfair to Vanessa about giving up Sunday School, but which one of them was truly serving the church and the Lord? Vanessa had shown great generosity, not only by spending all that money but by doing it without credit. Meanwhile, Mitzi had been grumbling and considering herself superior because she worked so hard as a volunteer. And there were so many Sundays when she didn't even get to church!

Right then and there, she vowed to make a change. She would no longer judge people. Vanessa had served in a different way, that's all, and, to tell the truth, Mitzi admired people who could say no.

In the future, if a teacher couldn't come, Mitzi would combine classes and make sure she herself got to church. She didn't know how much longer she would be in charge of the Sunday School, but she would try to do a better job of it.

She lifted her voice in song.

The Slob Who Was Robbed

1974

"...burglary, Mrs. Franklin. Robbery involves personal contact with the victim. These kids broke into your house when you weren't here, so it's burglary."

I looked at the badge on his blue uniform. Canaday.

"How do you know they were kids, Officer Canaday?" I asked.

"Well, your TV and stereo are still here. Kids don't know how to fence things. They were probably looking for cash. Did you have any around?"

My husband Greg spoke up. "Just the grocery money, right, Marilyn? Upstairs in my nightstand."

He led the second policeman to our bedroom while I accompanied Officer Canaday on his inspection of the first floor.

"Here's where they came in," Canaday said, picking up clumps of mud from the pale blue carpet in the small bedroom that Greg and I hoped to turn into a nursery someday. Right now it was the place where things without a place ended up. Suitcases were piled in one corner; the empty boxes which had stored the Christmas decorations all year now were scattered around the room. The closet was filled with summer sandals and deflated beach balls.

Canaday tried the window and raised it easily.

"But I'm sure that window was locked!" I protested.

"Windows in these old houses are a piece of cake, even for kids. Take my advice, Mrs. Franklin. Talk to a locksmith about locks to prevent the windows from being raised. Or, you could get burglar bars."

It was the Sunday between Christmas and New Year's. Greg and I had eaten brunch downtown with his parents and then had gone to a movie. Great brunch, so-so movie, and now this! I pictured two faceless teenagers wandering through my house, looking in my drawers, touching my things. I felt like I'd been punched in the stomach.

"Now, that's strange," Canaday said.

"What?"

"Well, it looks like they were going to take your crockpot and then changed their minds. They left it here in the middle of the floor."

"No, er…actually, that's where it is all the time. I mean, that's where I keep it."

The policeman looked at me and raised one eyebrow.

"Well, I got it last summer, it's too hot to use the oven in summer, and there's no room for it in the kitchen, and I haven't decided where to keep it, so…"

"So you keep it in the middle of the bedroom floor?"

"It seemed like a good idea at the time," I muttered.

I followed Canaday into the pantry, one of my favorite rooms because I love to cook. There were six wide, deep shelves. I had intended to categorize the groceries somehow, maybe dessert things on one shelf, vegetables on another. But time always slipped away, and the shelves were a mess. Cracker boxes lay on their sides, cans of tuna sat next to boxes of cereal. The lack of organization never really bothered me, and it drove Greg nuts that I could always put my hands on whatever I needed. But standing there next to this stranger, knowing what he probably thought of my housekeeping, I began to feel defensive.

A voice called from upstairs, "Canaday! Get up here."

The policeman started up the stairs, carefully stepping over two piles of laundry. I picked up one and followed him.

"They got the grocery money all right," the second officer said, pointing to Greg's open drawer.

"How much was in there?" Canaday asked Greg.

"About $100."

"Well, if that's all they took, consider yourselves lucky."

I watched as they surveyed the room. Greg's nightstand held the alarm clock and a book he had been reading. Mine held my Bible, stuffed with pieces of paper with prayer chain requests, and several magazines and paperbacks and half a bag of potato chips.

The two policemen opened Greg's closet and walked inside. All the suits were on one side, shirts and trousers on the other, everything sorted by color and hung with buttons facing the door. Shoes were in racks, tennis shoes together, loafers, dress shoes. It looked like an ad for a company that would come in and organize your closets.

Then Canaday crossed the room and opened my closet door. He whistled.

"Wow! They really went through here!"

Shoes and purses were scattered willy-nilly. A couple of skirts hung by only one of the two hooks on their hangers. A blue chenille bathrobe had fallen to the floor. One sleeve of a red plaid jacket was inside out.

"Anything missing here?" he asked me.

I pretended to search and then shook my head.

As the officers went downstairs, I looked over at Greg, who was biting his lower lip to keep from laughing.

"Thanks," I whispered.

"For what?"

"For not telling them that my closet always looks like that."

Mint Jelly

1980

On Thursdays they cleaned the streets near the Rutgers University Library, and everyone had to find places for their cars in the park.

On a February morning, Maureen Donovan grumbled as she pulled into a space. How could they possibly clean the streets when the snow was falling an inch every two hours?

A red Mustang with Louisiana license plates pulled in front of her. As she got out of her Pinto, she called out to the driver, "I'll bet you wish you were back home."

The tall blond with wire-rimmed glasses walked with her to the Library. His name was Alex LeBlanc, and he was a graduate student. She told him that she was one of the reference librarians and that if he ever needed any help, be sure to call on her.

A week later, Maureen saw him in the lobby of the Library.

He acted surprised to see her and asked if she'd like to go for a cup of coffee. She arranged to meet him in twenty minutes, then raced to the ladies' room and combed her short brown hair, which luckily she had washed just that morning. The azure sweater brought out the blue of her eyes, and she was satisfied with her appearance.

Later, Roger, the security guard, told her that the young man had been hanging around for about an hour before she came along, and afterward he asked Roger what her name was because he had forgotten.

Maureen didn't discover until months later that Alex's New Year's resolution was to meet a girl, but she thanked Heaven for him every chance she got. As spring came and went, she found herself falling in love with him.

She took him home to meet her family in Scranton. He fit in easily, sitting in the kitchen eating Mom's cherry pie and putting his feet up on the worn hassock Papa refused to let Salvation Army haul away. Alex never complained when their old dog jumped up and slobbered all over him. He slept on a cot in her brother David's room because their small house didn't have a guest room. There was one more person to use the single bathroom, but they all managed that long weekend.

Maureen and Alex spent a lovely summer going on picnics and taking drives at night to the seashore, the very best time to go to avoid the crowds. They enjoyed being together and had much in common. Years later neither would be able to remember who first said "I love you" or the circumstances.

Maureen found a fondue pot in a garage sale in September and got a cookbook from the library. They made cheese fondue and drank a great quantity of white wine, so when Alex said, "Why don't we get married?" she told him to ask her again the next day when they were completely sober.

To her delight, he did ask again, and, of course, she said yes.

In October Alex announced that his parents were going to be in New Jersey for two days on their way home from London. He suggested that Maureen get to know them before he told them the news.

The LeBlancs invited Alex and Maureen to join them for dinner at the hotel that first night. She was understandably frightened of meeting Alex's mother, who proved to be gracious and elegant, so elegant that

Maureen began to wish that she had not already invited them to her apartment for dinner the following night. Alex's father was funny and down-to-earth.

She got through the first night, one more to go.

As she awaited her guests, she looked at her apartment, trying to see it through their eyes. Alex had always liked the way she decorated it, bright colors and huge throw pillows. When the two of them ate there, they sat on the carpet in the living room and ate from the coffee table. For that night she had borrowed a neighbor's card table, four chairs, and a square tablecloth.

Dinner turned out well; it was a chicken dish she had made for Alex many times. She called his parents Captain and Mrs. LeBlanc, and they didn't suggest otherwise.

She had made it through the second night.

Alex told her later that he drove his parents to the airport, sat with them in the gate area making small talk, and then, just as they got up to board, said as casually as he could manage, "By the way, Maureen and I are going to get married when I graduate."

Maureen spent Christmas with her family and then on December 27 flew to New Orleans for a week with the LeBlancs.

Alex was waiting at the gate, looking more handsome than ever, if that were possible, and she flew into his arms. They collected her luggage and headed for his home.

Maureen had a feeling of foreboding as they pulled into the driveway of a huge brick house with a magnolia tree in front that nearly reached the roof.

Once inside her heart began to pound. Antiques everywhere, a real dining room with eight chairs, Wedgewood china (she peeked when no one was looking), crystal, sterling silver, fresh flowers in the middle of winter. She remembered her own home and wondered what Alex must have thought, remembered her eclectic apartment and these people, her future in-laws, eating from a card table, for Heaven's sake. How was she ever going to fit in with this family?

While Mrs. LeBlanc put the finishing touches on dinner and chatted with Alex, his father took Maureen through the entire house, showing her his souvenirs from thirty years in the Navy, medals and plaques, pictures of himself with the King of Thailand. She learned that he had grown up on a small farm in the Midwest, in a family not unlike her own. He was easy to talk to, and she began to relax. Things would turn out well after all.

They sat down to dinner. There were more forks and knives and spoons than Maureen had expected, but she just kept looking across the table at Alex to see what he would use. They were drinking champagne since this was a special occasion, but she made sure not to drink too much, didn't want to do or say anything foolish.

The main course was a leg of lamb, something Maureen's mother had never made at home. It looked delicious.

Captain LeBlanc handed Maureen the mint jelly, which was in a silver and crystal dish. He held it by the handle at the top and with his other hand on the bottom, but Maureen, thinking it was all one piece, simply took it by the handle.

As she did, the crystal dish of green jelly went flying through the air and landed upside down on the gold carpet between her and Alex's mother.

It was as though the moment were frozen in time. Everyone stared at the mess she had made, then Alex and his mother both jumped up and went into the kitchen for paper towels and carpet stain remover.

They seemed to be gone a very long time. Perhaps Mrs. LeBlanc was telling Alex that if he had any ideas of marrying such a klutz, he could forget it.

Maureen had visions of flying back home that very night. Her eyes filled with tears, and she sank lower and lower in her chair.

Captain LeBlanc caught her eye, and he was smiling. He took a bite of his lamb, put down his fork, lifted his glass, and took a sip.

"I know how you feel," he said with a grin. "Keep eating."

Postscript: The carpet stain came out, Maureen and Alex were married the following summer, the LeBlancs turned out to be warm and wonderful in-laws and lived near Maureen and Alex for many years. Maureen and her father-in-law adored each other, and the much-repeated story of the mint jelly, to her chagrin, became a family tradition.

The Fruit of Her Labors

1996

Marilee Spencer looked at her watch. In six hours Justin would be home.

His favorite dinner was in the crockpot, fresh sheets and a clean quilt were on his bed, the Christmas tree was up and decorated. Gifts had been bought and wrapped. Now there was nothing to do but wait.

She entered his room and chuckled out loud as she noticed that his telephone answering machine, which she had just turned on last night, already registered three messages.

She looked around the room. So many memories. Trophies. Photographs. So much of her life was reflected in this, her son's bedroom.

Marilee had chosen to be a stay-at-home mother. All during her pregnancy she had weighed her options: to stay at home with the baby or to work full-time at her public relations job and depend on day care. Even as they wheeled her into the delivery room, she hadn't decided. But the day after Justin was born, as she nursed him in the rocking chair, her heart filled with such love as she had never imagined, and she knew that she would never be able to leave him with someone else.

She had filled her days with caring for her husband and only child and with volunteer work, being team mother for soccer, Little League, and Pop Warner football. She had been on the PTA Board for six years, had served as director of the Sunday School at their church, and had driven for Meals on Wheels during the day while Justin was in school. Her husband Jack was wonderful, never allowing her to feel that what she was doing was unimportant. And Jack's parents always proudly told their friends that Justin had turned out so well because Marilee had stayed home with him.

It hadn't always been easy. Some of the mothers of Justin's friends seemed defensive around her, others condescending as though she sat around all day while they held important jobs. Marilee would never forget the time she had accompanied Jack to a business dinner and then discovered that he had to sit on the dais while she was placed at a table with people she didn't know. The man on her left had asked, "And which company do you work for?" She had started to tell him about her volunteer work, but he soon turned to the person on his other side, and no one talked to Marilee for the rest of the meal. Years later, when she discovered the term "networking", she realized why. There was nothing she could do for them.

It had been particularly hard on Marilee when Justin began to think seriously about college. On the one hand, she wished that he would go to one of the local schools, so he could live at home. But she realized that Jack was right; their son needed the experience of being away, of living in a different part of the country. Some of her friends, whose children went to UCLA and USC, told her that they didn't see their children very much, despite their being just hours away from San Diego.

Marilee had prayed that Justin would be guided to the right school, and in the end he had decided to go to Creighton University in Omaha, mostly because of their policy of giving preference to their own graduates for entry into the professional schools.

Now, at Christmas in his sophomore year, he was just about one-third of the way through college.

The first year had been somewhat hard on Justin.

He didn't have to study very hard in high school and still made good grades in honors courses. His first semester grades in college weren't bad, though, and the second semester he did even better.

His going off to college was hardest on Marilee. Suddenly she had so little to do. There were no football games to go to, no basketball games to run the concession stand for. One day Jack came home with an interesting bit of news: there was an opening in the public relations office at one of the universities in the city. He encouraged her to apply, and, surprisingly, she got the job.

Having Justin away meant more time to be with Jack, and Marilee found herself falling in love with him all over again. She guiltily wondered if he had felt neglected all those years, and she silently vowed to make it up to him.

She wanted to make this the perfect Christmas, for surely the day would come when Justin would not be with them for the holiday. When he married, there would be another family to compete for his presence.

Lately Marilee found herself with conflicting emotions. She wanted her son to be independent, to be able to make it on his own, and yet it hurt a little to think that he didn't need her anymore. She didn't want to be the kind of mother who would put demands on him and his wife and their children, yet she couldn't imagine a Christmas without him. This, she decided, was the most difficult period in all of her years as a mother. Jack had pointed out that it was also the most rewarding, for she was seeing the fruit of all her labors of love.

Justin's flight was on time, but he was not among the first off the plane. In fact, Marilee, biting her lower lip, began to worry. Reading her thoughts, Jack laughed and said, "He didn't miss it."

She thought back to another flight sixteen years earlier, when she had been the one coming back and her child the one waiting at the airport. She and Jack had gone ahead to prepare their new home in San Diego, and Justin had stayed behind for a week in Pittsburgh with his grandparents. The flight had seemed never-ending, the people in the aisle in front of her so slow gathering their things and getting off the plane. As soon as she could break free, she had bolted and run toward the area where people waited for incoming passengers. Later she realized that she probably had been discourteous in her frantic rush to see her boy. But what a joy to see him, waving his little hand and pulling Grandpa toward her.

Justin was the last, the very last, off the plane. He'd put on a few pounds, looked taller, had let his hair grow.

"Hi, Mom," he said nonchalantly after kissing her cheek, as though he had seen her yesterday.

They went home for dinner, and then later he went out with his friends. It was a pattern familiar from other recent visits. He would sleep late, play basketball or golf, come home for dinner and a few hours in the evening, and then go out again.

This time, however, when Marilee reached into the hamper for his dirty clothes to wash, she found it empty. When she came back from the grocery store, she saw Justin ironing a dress shirt. And he made his own sandwiches for lunch, plus one for her.

On Christmas Eve the three of them went to church. Afterward, Marilee put the finishing touches on the breakfast casserole she would pop into the oven when she got up in the morning. As she went down the hall toward her bedroom, she paused and knocked on Justin's door.

He sat on the floor at the foot of his bed, playing Nintendo. She sat down beside him.

"Glad to be home?" she asked for perhaps the twentieth time.

"Uh-huh," he said with a smile.

"Can I ask you something?"

He hesitated. "Okay, but I have a feeling you aren't going to ask which juice I want for breakfast."

"Are you content with your life?"

"Sure, Mom. Of course!"

"Are you <u>happy</u>?"

He looked at her and smiled. "Very."

"So you think Creighton was the right choice?"

"Sure."

"And what about being on your own?"

He grinned and patted her hand as he said, "I <u>love</u> it!"

She kissed him and walked down the hall. Jack was right, this was the time for seeing the fruit of her labors, and it was good.

45745268R00115

Made in the USA
Middletown, DE
12 July 2017